"At the beginning of this book Da\     ...cy introduces us to the Immanuel Factor, 'God with us.' That phrase becomes the basis for studying many heroes in the Bible who experienced the presence of God. Read *Living in His Presence* to have your life changed. As I've often said, It's not so much that you touch God; you must also let God touch you."

> Elmer L. Towns, Vice President and
> Dean of the School of Religion
> Liberty University

"*Living in His Presence* is a great encouragement for Christians to seek the presence of God in a fresh way. Practical and engaging, this book provides insightful guidance on how to develop your relationship with God."

> Rich Nathan, Senior Pastor
> Vineyard Church of Columbus

DAVE EARLEY is the founding pastor of New Life Church in Columbus, Ohio, a congregation of two thousand, as well as the creator of the New Life Center for Church Growth, Health, and Multiplication. He has written several books, including *Eight Habits of Effective Small Group Leaders* and *The 21 Most Effective Prayers of the Bible*.

Dave and his wife, Cathy, enjoy hiking, biking, and hanging out with their three teenage sons, Daniel, Andrew, and Luke. They make their home in Ohio.

# DAVE EARLEY

# LIVING in HIS PRESENCE

## The Immanuel Factor

BETHANY HOUSE PUBLISHERS
*Minneapolis, Minnesota*

Published by Bethany House Publishers
11400 Hampshire Avenue South
Bloomington, Minnesota 55438

Bethany House Publishers is a division of
Baker Publishing Group, Grand Rapids, Michigan.

Printed in the United States of America

**Library of Congress Cataloging-in-Publication Data**

Earley, Dave, 1959–
    Living in His presence : the Immanuel factor / Dave Earley.
       p.  cm.
    Summary; "'Living in His Presence' explores the Immanuel Factor in the lives of Bible characters—that moment when they knew God was with them and their lives were forever changed. The book's accessible and faith-stretching message speaks to new and seasoned Christians alike"—Provided by publisher.
    Includes bibliographical references.
    ISBN 0-7642-0070-4 (pbk.)
    1. Jesus Christ—Presence.  2. Christian life.  I. Title.
BT590.P75E27    2005
232—dc22

                                                 2005019817

*I dedicate this book*
*to the people of New Life Church.*
*I see God on your faces*
*and feel Him through your lives.*

*Thank you.*

## Acknowledgments

Every successful project is the result of a team effort. Together everyone accomplishes more. This book is no exception. At the risk of leaving someone out, I want to express my gratitude to many who played a role in this book's completion.

Cathy, you are a wonderful wife. I have seen God on your face since the first time we prayed together. You grow more beautiful every day.

Daniel, Andrew, and Luke, you are awesome sons. I am so proud of each of you. Thanks for praying for me and giving me so much joy.

Kyle Duncan. Thanks for being a risk taker, for believing in me, and for having such a strong passion to sponsor communicators of the deeper things of God.

Jeanne Hedrick. You are an answer to prayer, a wise voice of reason, and an outstanding editor. Thank you very much for all of your hard work.

Susan Chittum. What an amazing help and an awesome proofreader! Thanks.

Jack Hayford. You were the first to explain the differing levels of the presence of God in a way that turned the light bulbs on in my head.

Elmer Towns. This book would never have been written without your example and sponsorship. Thank you so much.

Norm Rohrer. Thank you for your mentoring.

Les Stobbe. Your CWG lessons on nonfiction liberated me to write the way my heart was leading. You are awesome.

The ministry staff of New Life Church. Your Wednesday morning insights on this material enriched my ability to understand and apply these truths.

Thanks to Aunt Florence, Mom and Dad, Keith, Joyce, Andy, Mikki, Kathy, Connie, Marilyn, Rick and Debbie, Laurie, Kristy, Tina, Ken Freeman, the Wednesday Night Bible Study group, Sonja, Jack, Carol, and Teresa. I deeply appreciate your examples and thank you for letting me tell your stories.

# Contents

# Prologue

*"If I could only ever give you one thing, it would be . . . God.*
*If you could only choose one thing, you should choose . . . God.*
*The very best of all things is . . . God.*
*With God you have all things.*
*Without God you have nothing."*

A FTER DAYS OF PRAYER and fasting, I stood in front of several thousand eager college students, and those were the words that came out. I had planned on saying something else, something funny and entertaining. But all I could talk about was God.

"You need God.
Revival is God.
It's all about God."

God made an appearance on that campus. We spent the next couple of days basking in the magnificent glory of the manifest presence of God. All-night prayer meetings broke out, students swarmed the altars, lives were turned right side up, young people were called to ministry, young men and women confessed Christ as Savior, and discouraged leaders were refreshed—all because of the manifest presence of God.

Those involved had some unspeakably wonderful and personal God-moments. An example of such a moment occurred one night as I was speaking. It was as though I could see the glory of God, like thousands of brilliant, sparkling, golden lights, falling as gently as snowflakes down on the students. The holy hush on the audience was only broken as students began to weep. It was warmly sweet and precious to feel God in the room loving His children. And He loves you in the same way. He wants you to deeply experience Him. You can. You absolutely must.

This is a book about revival. It is a study of changed lives. It is a manual in spiritual formation and a primer on discipleship. It is about protection, power, peace, and promotion. It is a guide to blessing. It contains ancient secrets to contemporary problems. It is all that and more, but only because it is about God.

Be honest. Do you ever wish that you:

◆ had a much closer relationship with God?
◆ loved God so much that you could resist irresistible temptations?
◆ could overcome fear?
◆ were changed to be a lot more like Jesus?
◆ had the power to do greater things to make a difference for God's kingdom?
◆ saw God defeat the enemy when he tried to attack you?
◆ had so much of God in your life that other people could not help but notice?
◆ were able to maintain a high-level walk with God, no matter what?

Have you ever asked:

◆ How can I really experience God?
◆ Why do some Christians seem to live under the smile of God's favor and others don't?
◆ How is it that some people come through adversity more blessed than before?
◆ Where do some people get their burning passion for God?
◆ Is there a simple secret to the effective Christian life that I am missing?
◆ Is there a set of activities that are simple, attainable, and realistic enough that I can apply them to my daily life and live a more fruitful Christian life?

I have asked these questions. So have many others. There is good news: The Bible contains the answers to these questions. The purpose of this book is to share the discovery with you, so you can enjoy your own wild ride in the adventure that is God.

INTRODUCTION:

# THE POWER RELEASED

IT WAS ONE OF THE WILDEST RIDES of my life.
Spring had finally broken and the weather was perfect.
Leaves burst open and birds sang of their delight to be alive. A
wonderful warm calm hung in the clear blue sky.

My son Andrew and I had only been kayaking a few times
before and always down the relatively tame waters of Big Walnut
Creek. Typically its waters meandered along at a fairly calm
pace, but not today. Even though it hadn't rained all week, we
were pleasantly surprised that the creek was unusually high and
the water was moving extremely fast.

Traveling more than twice as fast as usual, our two-man
kayak tilted and rocked through the rough spots. Still new to
kayaking, we felt proud that we had gone almost the whole way
without tipping.

Then suddenly the speed of the waters accelerated frantically
as we careened through a narrow section. We maintained our
balance and lurched forward, struggling to stay in control. Unex-
pectedly, the creek split in two as the high waters shot over the
banks and through the woods. Sucked sideways into a jumble of
broken branches, we found ourselves leaning away from the
sharp points of the jagged branches. As the rushing water
bounced off the branches it threw our boat back, and we tipped
over into the chaotic caldron of wild water.

It took everything we had to rescue the boat, dump the
water out, and finish our ride. It had been quite an adventure—

one we would not forget. And it sure beat sitting home watching TV.

We gained a new respect for the power of high water in the creek. We also learned to be extra careful when kayaking in water that had just been freed from a dam.

Hoover Memorial Reservoir feeds Big Walnut Creek just a few miles upstream from where we put in our boat. Hoover is the major water source for hundreds of thousands of people living in and around Columbus, Ohio. We had not realized it when we put our kayak in, but the water authorities had briefly opened Hoover, releasing a mighty surge of additional water. The inrush of hundreds of gallons of water per second caused the stream flow to increase several thousand cubic feet per second. The unleashing of so much water all at once transformed a placid creek into a raging torrent, turning a peaceful float into a memorable adventure.

Since then I have a new appreciation for the potential power residing just a couple of miles upstream in Hoover Reservoir. A brief release of just a small percentage of the vast amount of water in that large lake mightily transformed Big Walnut Creek.

So it is with God. To us, He often seems to be a large placid lake, resting just off in the distance. But when just a bit of His presence is released to flow in us and through us, the results are astounding. God's manifest presence with us is the most misunderstood and underutilized power source in the universe.

God is dangerous, mysterious, surprising, amazing, mind-bending, and life-changing. God is eternal, all-powerful, wise, mighty, loving, and very smart. He is wild, real, and really, really good. When you can hang out with Him, good things cannot help but happen in your life. God is great, gracious, and generous. When He is near us, we become candidates to experience the blessings that follow in His wake.

Applying the Immanuel Factor can lead you into a much deeper, more vivid relationship with God than you have ever known. It is a lifestyle that positions you to encounter much more of God than you thought possible. It helps you begin to live the life you have inwardly longed for and to be the person you have always wanted to be. It is enjoying such a God-saturated interior life that your exterior life shines as a result. The manifest presence of God—it is so simple. It is so powerful. It is so practical. It is so available. It is so underutilized and misunderstood. When it is released, it can make your life a wild and wonderful ride.

### CHAPTER ONE

# God With Us
## The Immanuel Factor

---

*Forty-eight percent of regular church attenders have not experienced God's presence in the past year.*

—GEORGE BARNA[1]

---

A COUPLE OF YEARS AGO I grappled with the gnawing realization that *something was missing.* I had been a highly committed follower of Jesus for over twenty years, yet deep inside there was something severely amiss.

Twenty years earlier I had traded falling down drunk with homemade wine for being madly in love with God (Ephesians 5:18). He became my joy, my anchor, my buddy, my Savior. I loved everything about Him. The highlight of my day was our hour-long rendezvous, when I would pour out my heart into His listening ears. His presence was my magnificent obsession. I wildly relished just being with Him.

Yet now I missed Him.

I understood that God often withdraws a sense of His presence for a time in order to help us mature in our faith. But this was more than that. This was not a dark season of the soul; it was a long, lonely rut of desert desperation.

Too busy in the ministry while raising a family, I had begun relating to God purely from my head and will, not out of the wellspring of a heart on fire. Even though I was still strong in my faith, I was appalled to catch myself going through spiritual routines and whipping out prayers by rote. I realized that the flames of my "first love" were dangerously low.

The holy hunger and desperation to know God had cooled. That aching urgency to be with God had left. I knew I had to have something more than merely going through the motions and doing the right thing—I must have God himself.

I knew that no one-time emotional experience was the answer. No. What I had to have was a deeper encounter with God in both my mind and my emotions and a greater sense of God's presence in my daily life. But I wasn't sure what to do.

Then I remembered the Immanuel Factor.

### Ohio Earley

Years earlier, as a college student, I set out to read all the way through the Bible in a year. My goal was to follow the three-chapters-a-day-will-keep-the-devil-away plan.

As I opened my Bible every day I felt like a spiritual Indiana Jones—or in this case, Ohio Earley. I approached God's Word with a consuming sense of awesome anticipation. I was sure that delightful discoveries were just on the horizon. I loved the adventure of reading for myself the famous stories, popular promises, and timeless truths I had heard many times before. I also enjoyed "discovering" wonderful Bible events or insights I did not know existed.

As I read through the Old Testament I noticed something. Nestled in the defining events of almost every great Bible character was the little phrase "God was with him." This was something I could not remember hearing anyone preach on or teach about. But there it was, regularly repeated in the Scriptures. One hero after another was said to be blessed or successful because of one common denominator: "The Lord was with him."

Then I came to the New Testament book of Matthew. After wading through the genealogies, I was pleased to pop out into the Christmas story (Matthew 1:18–25). Again, I noticed something new to me. As you know, an angel told Joseph that the baby Mary was carrying was the most legit baby ever conceived. The baby even had a title. The messenger angel quoted the prophet Isaiah, "'The virgin will be with child and will give birth to a son, and they will call him Immanuel'—which means, 'God with us'" (Matthew 1:23).

I had heard and read that before, of course, but this time I saw that last phrase with fresh eyes. I slowly read the familiar words again, "They will call him 'Immanuel,' which means, 'God with us.'"

"God with us." That was the concept I had noticed throughout the Old Testament—God's blessed presence with mankind. Jesus could be referred to as Immanuel because He was to be God present with us. From that point on, I began to think of the active presence of God with us as "Immanuel" and to call the reality of experiencing the manifest presence of God "the Immanuel Factor."

As I reminisced about the early years of my spiritual walk the phrase "God with me" struck a chord. That was what I remembered. I loved that warm smile of God shining on my face and the strong hand of God guiding my life. It was flat-out fun to be with God and to know He was with me, *really* with me.

I missed Him. I longed for that "God is with me" experience again.

I began to read back through the Old Testament just to make sure that the Immanuel Factor was really there. Yep. Immanuel, God's presence, was frequently cited as the determining factor in the success and failure of the people of God. I noticed that it was not indiscriminately given, though. There were prerequisites for experiencing the manifest presence of God and conditions that would lead to the noticeable decrease of His presence as well.

As this came together in my mind a fire began to build in my heart. My pulse pounded with the same adrenaline that must have raced through the veins of Christopher Columbus when he stood on the shores of the New World, or in Lewis and Clark when they saw the Pacific Ocean. I was on to something. I really *was* Ohio Earley. I had stumbled onto an ancient treasure. In the Immanuel Factor I had discovered a forgotten secret of spiritual success. I held a key that could unlock the door to a deeper encounter with God and gain access to the vast storehouse of spiritual riches.

Then I began to rummage through some biographies of great men and women of God. If this is real, I figured, they must have seen it too—and applied it to their lives. The first few books I yanked down from my shelves were the stories of Corrie ten Boom, Amy Carmichael, John Wesley, D. L. Moody, Charles Spurgeon, and Charles Finney. Bing! Bang! Bong! Boom! Every one of them evidenced the Immanuel Factor! This could be big.

Next, I worked back through the New Testament to see if, and how, the Immanuel Factor applies today under the new covenant. I found the Immanuel Factor to be central in the new covenant. The principles sketched in the lives of the Old Testament saints were fleshed out and applied by the Spirit-filled life described in the New Testament.

## WHAT IS THE IMMANUEL FACTOR?

The term *Immanuel Factor* may seem a bit fuzzy. Let me attempt to clarify it somewhat up front, and then we will unpack it as we go. When I speak of the Immanuel Factor, I am speaking of a *heightened experience of the manifest presence of God.* I am talking about an increased capacity to be in step with the Almighty and move in the sphere of His activity.

While available to everyone at salvation, the Immanuel Factor is not realized or applied by every Christian because there are choices that need to be made and conditions that need to be met. This book is a study of those key requirements that *release* the manifest presence of God in our lives.

The Immanuel Factor can produce anything (or everything) that could be expected by keeping close company with God. God's manifest presence may result in evident blessing, inner transformation, even outright miracles—but it will not necessarily do so.

Ironically, as I write this book, I am in a season of affliction. My friends jokingly call me "Job." Even though I am not *feeling* much of the presence of God, I can still see Him very actively at work in the midst of my adversity. I know that in a few years I will see His fingerprints all over this season of sorrow.

The recipients of the Immanuel Factor are usually keenly aware of it, but that's not always the case. There are times when we only see the presence of God through the lens of hindsight. Looking back, it becomes abundantly clear that He was very close to us and highly active on our behalf.

### Immanuel Means "God With Us"

As we have seen, *Immanuel* is a Hebrew word that means "God with us" (Matthew 1:23). Those three words serve as the foundation, core, and climax of the Immanuel Factor. Each word is crammed full of meaning. Let's look at each of them in turn.

#### GOD

Immanuel means "*God* with us." The Immanuel Factor is living with a heightened experience and awareness of the manifest presence of God. The beauty of the Immanuel Factor is that it is not primarily about us. It is about God. Maybe you wanted to read this book because you were looking for something that seemed to be missing from your daily life. That something is Someone—God! What you really crave is found by experiencing more of Him—more often, more deeply, more intimately, and more powerfully—than you imagined possible.

#### WITH

Immanuel means "God *with* us." The Immanuel Factor is living with a heightened experience and awareness of the manifest presence of God. The Immanuel Factor is God's presence with us in a tangible, potent way.

You may be thinking, "But isn't God with us all the time anyway?" The answer is yes and no. We need to distinguish the difference between the four levels of the presence of God. The first level is what theologians call *omnipresence*. It means that God is everywhere present and present everywhere. He is infinite; therefore, He is present in all places at the same time. The omnipresence of God touches everyone and everything in the universe.

It is kind of like air. It is always there, but we pay little attention to it—unless for some reason it is suddenly removed.

The second level of God's presence could be called the *abiding* presence of God. The Bible describes the abiding presence of God when it says, "'Never will I leave you; never will I forsake you'" (Hebrews 13:5). It is a promise believers enjoy because it gives us such sweet comfort. It only touches the followers of God.

It is like the sun. Prior to meeting God through faith in Christ, our souls only knew darkness or night. But after meeting God, our eyes were opened to the delights of the day and the sweet sensations of the sun. We are glad that God's abiding presence is always with us and are comforted by enjoying its warmth and light. After a while, though, we tend to take it for granted.

There is also a third level of God's presence. We could call it the *heavenly* presence of God. It affects those who are in heaven, where God's presence is revealed in an unlimited way. God's presence is unhindered and unrestricted there. Heaven is all God, all the time. That is what makes it so heavenly!

Because God is light (1 John 1:5), heaven is full of light (Revelation 21:23–25; 22:5). As God is creative, excellent, loving, joyful, encouraging, faithful, true, good, and holy, so is heaven a marvelously holy place, overflowing with all that is beautiful and truly excellent, running over with love, joy, encouragement, truth, and peace. Heaven is the sphere where the heavenly presence of God is unleashed.

So there is the omnipresence of God, the abiding presence of God, and the heavenly presence of God. But none of these are what we call the Immanuel Factor.

The Immanuel Factor is about experiencing the *manifest* presence of God. It is God's personality made obvious, tangible, and visible in us, around us, and for us. It is like walking in the sunshine, yet much more. It is God's creative, excellent, living, loving, joyful, encouraging, faithful, true, good, and holy presence flowing around and within us. It is having a distinctive aura of God punctuating and permeating everything about us. It is God at work in our lives.

### Us

Immanuel means "God with *us*." God is not a distant deity. He can become a close companion and an accessible ally. His presence is not something that is only offered to someone else. It is available to *us*—to me and to you.

The challenge of the Immanuel Factor is that choices we make can affect how much of the presence of God we enjoy. We can go through life blind to God, apprehending little of Him as His omnipresence goes largely unnoticed. We can become His children through faith in Jesus Christ and be comforted by His abiding presence, ultimately reveling in His heavenly presence.

But if we want to experience some measure of heaven on earth and we are willing to meet the conditions prescribed in the Word of God, then we can experience the *manifest* presence of God. God is available to all of us, but how much of God we experience and apprehend is up to us.

### What's He Doing?

We are privileged to have several dozen high school students gather in our home every Wednesday night to study the Bible. One night we talked about what it means to go through the day with a new awareness that God is *with you* at school. We talked about taking God with you as you walk through the halls, as you eat in the cafeteria, and as you go about your extracurricular activities. I was not sure if the students got it or not.

A few days later the wrestling team was at a large tournament. Keith, one of the wrestlers, had been at Bible study that week. As he walked out on the mat to wrestle a difficult opponent, I noticed that he had his right arm out and bent at a funny angle. It looked like he was escorting an invisible date.

I happened to be standing with some of the coaches and school administrators, watching the match, when Keith walked out with his invisible friend. One of them looked at him and muttered, "What's he doing?"

I gulped and rather shyly said, "I think he's taking God with him." They rolled their eyes and looked at me like I was not all there.

Keith proceeded to wrestle the best match of his life. When the referee lifted his hand at the end of the match, Keith put his arm around his invisible friend and walked off the mat with a silly grin on his face.

One of the coaches resignedly shook his head and said, "Well, whatever. I guess it works."

## Exploring the Immanuel Factor

In the next few chapters we will look at a variety of ways that God's presence affected many of the Bible heroes. We will learn what they did to cultivate their relationship with God and look at their awareness of and capacities for His presence. We will discover the ways that His manifest presence can be forfeited and the consequences that follow. We will observe the way the Immanuel Factor in the Old Testament is fully expressed by the Spirit-filled life in the New Testament. Finally, we will tie it all together by summarizing and applying the principles we have learned.

Join me on this expedition of discovery, insight, and adventure. During our trip we will see miraculous moments and daily blessings. We will see divine providence, promotion, public testimony, popularity, protection, potential, provision, power, and prosperity all flowing from the Immanuel Factor. Be prepared . . . the bountiful blessings and benefits will both stagger you and transform you. Our adventure will take us into parts of our lives that have long been concealed. But that's okay, because it will also lead us to God.

I am not an expert on the Immanuel Factor, just a fellow traveler. But I do have the map. So if you are ready, let's begin.

## Getting the Most From This Book

1. Offer a brief prayer as you start reading. Ask God to reveal himself and His truth to you through His Word. Remember that God is present to guide you.

2. Read one chapter at a sitting, and try to apply the Immanuel Factor principles to your life.
3. Read with a pen in hand. Underline sentences that jump out at you. Make notes in the margin.
4. Conclude each session of reading with a brief prayer. The goal is to draw closer to God.

### Applying This Chapter

1. Be alert. God is with you already. Open the eyes of your heart, and be aware of what He is doing in and around you.
2. Make the effort to consciously envision God's presence with you throughout the day.

# 14 Keys
*to* Releasing
*the* Manifest
Presence
*of* GOD

### CHAPTER TWO:

# Don't Leave Home Without Him

*Fervent Petition*

O NE DAY I HAD A LUNCH ENGAGEMENT with a testy church officer. I had asked him to meet with me to discuss some important issues. Over the meal I had to tell him that his suggestions for the new budget had not been accepted. I also shared some serious words of rebuke about his consistently critical attitude. My message was not well received.

When the waiter brought the bill, I reached into my pocket for my wallet. It was not there! I vainly searched one empty pocket after another. Vexation became absolute mortification when I realized that in my rush to get out of the house, I had left home without it.

So there I sat, being glared at by an extremely dejected, somewhat angry church officer as I fumbled unsuccessfully for a wallet that was at home on my dresser. This was not good.

I desperately wanted to die. That not being an option, I began to scheme. I could drop my napkin and get down under the table and crawl to freedom. But that wouldn't work, because he would see me. I could go to the bathroom and climb to liberty through the window, but I remembered that this restaurant had no windows in the rest room. I could pretend I was choking to death, which was not much of a stretch at this point, and hope that the bill would be forgotten in the chaos of my rescue.

But I had no guarantee the man glowering at me across the table would consider a rescue. Then what would I do?

So I had to humble myself, or more accurately, humiliate myself. I had to tell him that I had forgotten my wallet and ask him if he could cover the bill until I could pay him back the next day. I blushed deeply, winced, broke the bad news, and ducked. To his credit, he did not scream or yell. He quietly paid the bill and told me not to worry about paying him back. Boy, did that hurt. I wished he had hit me. Then I quietly slunk out to my car and made a promise: The next time I invite someone to lunch and have to give them bad news, I will make sure I have my wallet. There are some things that are so important you just can't leave home without them.

### Disaster in the Desert

I feel sorry for Moses. When we pick up his story, he is over eighty years old and is stuck in the desert with a million mewling people. Instead of sitting back to enjoy retirement, he was looking out for one of the most motley mobs of yahoos ever assembled. The Israelites had spent decades in slavery, so their new liberty quickly turned to license. Every time he turned around Moses found them either rebelling or griping.

On the heels of witnessing God's miracle of holding back the waters of the Red Sea so they could pass out of Egypt into freedom, they immediately whined about the drinking water. Then they wanted to make it very clear that they did not like the food. Then it was the water again. The complaining was constant.

When Moses marched down from Mount Sinai, carrying the tablets of truth that would guide them to national prosperity, he was astonished to find them worshiping a dumb idol in a wild, riotous party. The epitome of their ignorance was their claim that this newly fashioned idol was to be credited with delivering them from Egypt!

They were more than God could bear. He wanted to annihilate them. And He would have, had not Moses prayed for them. Even though God spared their lives, He said that He would no longer go with them (Exodus 33:3).

Moses felt the weight of the responsibility and the depth of the frustration of leading the Israeli nation safely to the Promised Land when they would have preferred to return to the familiar bondage of Egypt. Leading them was often like trying to herd cats. Guiding them safely through the hazards of the desert into the Promised Land without their destroying him or themselves seemed impossible.

So Moses prayed.

Men and women with great responsibilities either become people of prayer or they go nuts. History is littered with the sad stories of independent, self-sufficient leaders imploding under the strain of trying to lead people who refuse to be led. Fortunately, time also tells the tales of the God-dependent, praying remnant of leaders who succeeded in the task and lived to tell about it. Moses was such a leader. His power was prayer, and his prayers released the manifest presence of God on their behalf.

## PRINCIPLES OF THE IMMANUEL FACTOR

### 1. The presence of God is cultivated through regular meetings with God.

> Now Moses used to take a tent and pitch it outside the camp some distance away, calling it the "tent of meeting." Anyone inquiring of the LORD would go to the tent of meeting outside the camp. And whenever Moses went out to the tent, all the people rose and stood at the entrances to their tents, watching Moses until he entered the tent. As Moses went into the tent, the pillar of cloud would come down and stay at the entrance, while the LORD spoke with Moses. Whenever the people saw the pillar of cloud standing at the entrance to the tent, they all stood and worshiped, each at the entrance to his tent. The LORD would speak to Moses face to face, as a man speaks with his friend. (Exodus 33:7–11)

This passage contains three phrases that are especially helpful in our journey. They speak of the role of place, access, and friendship as foundational for God's manifest presence in Moses' life. Let's see what we can discover about the Immanuel Factor that we can apply to our own lives.

### A SPECIAL PLACE

"Moses used to take a tent and pitch it outside the camp some distance away, calling it the 'tent of meeting.'" Moses had a *place* where he met with God. It was away from the hustle of humanity. He went there to shut himself away from people so that he could shut himself away with God.

There is something special about having a particular place to meet God. When I first began to seek God as a high school student, I used to have a special place in the woods where I would go and meet with Him. There was a big fat dead tree lying on a small hill in the middle of nowhere. I never saw evidence of any human life near that tree, although deer walked by frequently and squirrels loved to play overhead. I used to lie on that tree, look up through the leaves at the sky, and pour my heart out to God.

During my first semester in college my special place with God was an operating room. Let me explain. My college was new and had not yet built dormitories. Instead, they rented an old hospital building downtown, where they housed male students. The only room that was not occupied by three or four young men was the operating room. I ran in at noon every weekday, locked the door, and met with God. I learned to sense the manifest presence of God in that place. At first an hour seemed like a long time. After a few days, however, it flew by, because *God was there*. Every day in that operating room Dr. Holy Spirit met with me and performed heart surgery.

A few years later I happened to be walking through that building and stopped in the operating room. As soon as I walked in the room my breath caught in my throat, my knees buckled, and I nearly sank to the floor as a spirit of prayer welled up within me. This had been my "tent of meeting." I had learned to love God there. I had to hurry out or risk embarrassing myself with a flood of tears. Such is the power of a special place to meet God.

## The Privilege of Access

"As Moses went into the tent, the pillar of cloud would come down." The pillar of cloud was the visible manifestation of the presence of God. It was Immanuel—God with them. When Moses went into the tent to meet God, He was there to meet Moses. God is always willing, ready, and available to meet with us when we make time for Him.

In those days only Moses enjoyed this direct, personal, and intimate access to the presence of God. Not so today! We all are invited to "come boldly to the throne of grace" (Hebrews 4:16 NKJV).

Often we think God is reluctant to meet with us. We have a mistaken notion that the whole time God is meeting with us He is rolling His eyes, looking at His watch, gazing out the window, and wondering when this encounter will be over so He can move on to other concerns. We think that the love He has for us is, at best, a has-to-tolerate-us love. Wrong! God loves us with a head-over-heels, absolutely-crazy-about, can't-wait-to-spend-time-with-us, wanting-it-to-last-a-little-longer type of love.

## The Privilege of Friendship

"The Lord spoke with Moses face to face, as a man speaks with his friend." Oh, to be a fly on the wall of that tent and overhear some of their conversations! Imagine talking with God face-to-face, as a man speaks with his friend! I wonder what God's voice sounded like to Moses. Were they always serious when they conversed, or did God sometimes tease Moses, like I tease my friends? Did Moses sometimes shake his head and ask God to explain women to him? I can't wait to get to heaven to find out the answers to these questions.

Moses employed the *privilege* of friendship available with God. He took full advantage of the access afforded him and met with God face-to-face. Nothing was hidden. It was a dear and open dialogue between friends.

The Immanuel Factor is all about God's presence, not His absence. It is the product of a close relationship. It is primarily about relationship, not rewards. In the next chapter we are going to examine this face-to-face friendship in great detail. For now it is enough to note that it is an essential ingredient for the Immanuel Factor to operate fully in our lives.

On the backside of the desert, during his forty years of exile, Moses developed a familiar friendship with God. That is the secret of Moses' inner strength. That is the foundation of effective prayer and the basis of experiencing the Immanuel Factor.

## 2. The manifest presence of God is released by specifically asking for it.

Moses knew by now that there was no way he could handle this assignment all by himself. Without God, it was impossible. It was too big. He was too small. Those he led were many; he was but one man. The obstacles were too numerous. Without God, all of it was a sad and tragic joke. The scorching heat and brutal barrenness of the desert, the persistent presence of warring enemies, the insatiable hunger of the masses for food, and their hunger for more freedom than they could handle would quickly devour and destroy them. Without God, it was a hopeless situation.

Moses needed divine accompaniment. He could not, would not, go on unless God went with him. There was no other way.

Stop.

Do you see the importance of this moment? Moses was overwhelmed and outflanked by potential problems. He was marching a million people through a minefield of imminent destruction. And fortunately, he was wise enough to know he could not make it without God. God's presence was not a nice addition or comforting accoutrement. It was the bottom-line essential.

Yet he not only recognized his desperate, gaping need; he *acted* on it. Moses was ultimately successful because he asked God for His presence.

> Moses said to the LORD, "You have been telling me, 'Lead these people,' but you have not let me know whom you will send with me. . . . Remember that this nation is your people." The LORD replied, "My Presence will go with you, and I will give you rest." Then Moses said to him, "If

your Presence does not go with us, do not send us up from here" (Exodus 33:12–15).

"If your Presence does not go with us, do not send us up from here." Moses' prime pursuit was the presence of God. When he could ask for one thing, he asked for that one thing—God's presence.

"Go with us." In other words, *I am not going without you. You are the key to our peace, protection, and prosperity. Your presence is the source of our survival and success. Without you, there will soon be none of us. So please, go with us.*

### The Necessity of a Reliable Guide

I have three teenage boys (which helps explain my prematurely gray hair). The four of us love the thrill of white water rafting. As far as we are concerned, the wilder the better . . . as long as we have a good guide. Guides know the river and the rapids, and they know the fine points of rafting. Having a guide is the prerequisite for us amateurs to navigate class-four rapids.

A few years ago we were rafting down one of the top rivers in North America in terms of the size of its rapids. We were stunned by the astounding beauty of the canyon around us and awed by the steep drops of the river below us. Sheer walls, over one thousand feet high, channeled the river wildly into narrow, unforgiving rapids in the midst of Royal Gorge. Excitedly, we pin-balled through rapids appropriately named "Sledgehammer" and "Boat Eater."

We were confidently enjoying the time of our lives because we had a good guide. At least we *had* a guide. When we got into the next set of rapids, we slammed headlong into a sharp boulder, launching him fifteen feet into the air and out of the boat! Panic-stricken, we knew we had no hope of facing the rest of the river and the danger of the rapids without our guide. It took an all-out effort to retrieve him from the bubbling brew of Hell's Kitchen and pull him back into the crazily careening boat. But we could not go on without him. We needed him to go with us.

Moses wisely realized how desperately he and the Israelites needed God to go with them. There was no way they could survive the wilderness without His presence. This is why Moses prayed, "If your Presence does not go with us, do not send us up from here." He recognized that in God's presence they would find His direction, protection, and provision. He also saw God's presence with them as their mark of distinction.

> "How will anyone know that you are pleased with me and with your people unless you go with us? What else will distinguish me and your people from all the other people on the face of the earth?" (Exodus 33:16).

There are some prayers God is more apt to answer than others. When we ask God for His presence, He responds.

> And the LORD said to Moses, "I will do the very thing you have asked, because I am pleased with you and I know you by name" (Exodus 33:17).

God did not rebuke him for this "selfish" prayer; He simply said yes. We don't ever have to be hesitant or embarrassed to ask God to go with us. The New Testament reminds us, "You do not have, because you do not ask God" (James 4:2).

### LET YOUR HAND BE WITH ME

Moses was not the only person to ask for God's presence. A fellow named Jabez offered a similar request.

> Jabez cried out to the God of Israel, "Oh, that you would bless me and enlarge my territory! Let your hand be with me, and keep me from harm so that I will be free from pain." And God granted his request. (1 Chronicles 4:10)

Notice those last five words: "And God granted his request." A straightforward request by Jabez was immediately answered by God. Asking Him to be with us is a prayer request God likes to answer.

## WRESTLING WITH THE LORD IN PRAYER

Moses and Jabez are not the only ones who found their heart-cry for Immanuel to be a life-changing prayer request. Many years later a man named Dwight became one of the most influential Christians of his generation. In a few short years he started a great church, an outstanding college, and two schools for orphaned boys. He is said to have introduced one million souls to Jesus Christ. He was a man who emanated the manifest presence of God.

But it was not always that way. Early in his ministry he was a highly dedicated man who tirelessly labored to try to bring souls, one by one, to Christ. A dear friend described him at this period of his life as "a great hustler; he had a tremendous desire to do something, but he had no real power. He worked very largely in the energy of the flesh."[1]

Dwight's heart was ignited to somehow reach more people for Christ than he was doing. He knew he wasn't up to the task, though. So he began to wrestle with the Lord in prayer. Two women convinced him that he needed an infusion of the powerful presence of God.

"There came a great hunger in my soul. I did not know what it was. I began to cry out as never before. I really felt that I did not want to live if I could not have this power for service."[2]

So he began to continually cry out for the powerful presence of God. Years later he shared what happened as a result.

> About four years ago I got into a cold state. It did not seem as if there was any unction [power] resting upon my ministry. For four long months God seemed to be just showing me myself. . . . But after four months the anointing came. It came upon me as I was walking in the streets of New York. Many a time I have thought of it since I have been here. At last I had returned to God again, and I was wretched no longer. I almost prayed in my joy, "O stay Thy hand!" I thought this earthen vessel would break. He filled me so full of the Spirit.
>
> If I have not been a different man since, I do not know myself. I think I have accomplished more in the last four

years than in all the rest of my life. The sermons were not different; I did not present any new truths; and yet hundreds were converted. I would not now be placed back where I was before that blessed experience if you should give me all the world—it would be as the small dust of the balance.[3]

Soon after this event, God gave Dwight L. Moody a global impact. The results of his efforts were incredibly multiplied. The only explanation is the manifest presence of God. Moody deeply, ardently, and passionately desired God's presence to go with him and consume his life. He made it a matter of serious prayer. And God answered in a mighty way.

### Five Tips for Improving Your Daily Time With God

◆ *Secure a private place.*
Unlike Moses, you probably won't use a tent. Your place may be a chair in the living room, a place at the dining room table, or on top of your bed. It may be in your car on the way to work or at your desk over lunch. Some talk with the Lord during their daily walk. *Where* it is is not as important as *that* it happens.

◆ *Establish a regular time.*
"Anytime" usually becomes no time. When we do not make appointments to meet with God, other things come at us and we get distracted. This is why many people meet with God first thing every morning to start their day.

◆ *Anticipate meeting with God.*
There is a difference between "having devotions" or "doing a quiet time" and connecting with the most awesome Person in the universe. Moses met with God, and so can we. Occasionally, dress up like you would to meet with the president or to go on a date. After all, God is more important than the president, and He loves you more than any date.

◆ *Speak your mind.*

Moses spoke with God as a friend. It was more than polite formalities and tired pleasantries. It was heart-to-heart and soul-to-soul.

◆ *Be specific.*

Moses did not beat around the bush or speak in vague generalities. He specifically asked, "Go with us" (Exodus 33:16). If we have specific needs, and we want definite answers, we need to make specific requests.

### CHAPTER THREE:

# No Matter What
*Resilient Loyalty*

AUNT FLORENCE HAD IT. There she sat, day after day, tiny and crumpled, a prisoner of her wheelchair. Her limbs were withered and crooked. Her joints gnarled and knotted by crippling rheumatoid arthritis. The joys and freedoms of daily life had long ago been taken from her. She could no longer take a walk across a field. She was incapable of bending down to scoop up a wiggling grandchild in her arms. She could not cook her family a big meal. She could not even get up and clean her little farmhouse.

Yet God shone all over her face.

Though she ached, in continual pain, you would never know it by measuring her smile. If the frustrations of bondage to the chair or the bed bothered her, she never complained of it. Her heart was not filled with self-pity or her countenance with sorrow. Resentment held no place in her heart. Instead, she sparkled with a deep and attractive joy.

She would literally light up when she spoke to me of the wonderful preachers she saw on TV. She peppered me with questions about the church that was born in our basement. When she told me that she prayed for me, I could tell she meant it. Her Bible had that wonderful worn look. And her clear blue eyes had that deep warmth of someone who knows a secret.

God gave Aunt Florence the desires of her heart. All four of her children grew up to live as committed Christians. Her son became a minister, and all her daughters married pastors. Her husband was a good and honest man. Even though rough through years of hard work, he was always very tender with her.

As I look back it is so obvious: Aunt Florence had the Immanuel Factor. Her relationship with God turned the prison of her wheelchair into a sweet sanctuary of solitude. In spite of and in the midst of her suffering, the glorious golden glow of God's presence shone all over her face and in her life.

It is possible through the Immanuel Factor to experience true prosperity in the midst of genuine adversity. It is possible to have God go with us through the fires of affliction and come out on the other side much better than the way we went in. Joseph will show us how.

### Joseph's Nightmare

Let's go back nearly four thousand years to the land of Egypt. As a young man, Joseph was given a dream that suggested he might become a ruler over his family. Yet at the age of seventeen he was jerked from his privileged life into a nightmare. Tricked by his older half brothers, he was shocked to see how they planned to murder him. He was only spared when they changed their minds and sold him as a slave to a caravan of people heading to Egypt. He ended up in bondage to Potiphar, the captain of Pharaoh's guard.

Joseph might have wondered if it would have been better if they had killed him. He went from being his father's favorite son to a nameless slave who had lost everything . . . everything, that is, but God. Let's pick the story up in Genesis:

> Now Joseph had been taken down to Egypt. Potiphar, an Egyptian who was one of Pharaoh's officials, the captain of the guard, bought him from the Ishmaelites who had taken him there. (Genesis 39:1)

There is nothing outstanding so far. There were thousands, maybe even millions, of slaves in Egypt. Joseph was just another one, except for one defining characteristic.

## The Lord Was With Him

*The* LORD *was with Joseph* and he prospered, and he lived in the house of his Egyptian master. When his master saw that *the* LORD *was with him* and that the LORD gave him success in everything he did, Joseph found favor in his eyes and became his attendant. Potiphar put him in charge of his household, and he entrusted to his care everything he owned. From the time he put him in charge of his household and of all that he owned, the LORD blessed the household of the Egyptian because of Joseph. The blessing of the LORD was on everything Potiphar had, both in the house and in the field. So he left in Joseph's care everything he had; with Joseph in charge, he did not concern himself with anything except the food he ate. (Genesis 39:2–6, emphasis added)

"The Lord was with Joseph." The Immanuel Factor was in effect for Joseph in a big way. God was with him. And good things resulted. "He prospered." Because God was with him, Joseph excelled as a slave doing backbreaking work out in the field. He did so well that he was moved inside to work in the house. God continued to be with him, and he was so successful working inside the house that his pagan Egyptian master took notice and gave Joseph the responsibility of being his personal attendant.

Because God was with Joseph, the blessing of God rested on everything he did. Potiphar's household was so blessed that Potiphar put Joseph in charge of everything he had. The nameless slave had become the right-hand man to the captain of Pharaoh's guard.

Certainly Joseph was bright. Obviously he worked very hard. As we will see in a moment, he was quite handsome. But when God recorded the story of Joseph, those factors were not mentioned as the reasons for his success. The reason he experienced such outlandish prosperity and incredible success was because *the Lord was with him.* Joseph was experiencing the manifest presence of God. He was a poster boy for the Immanuel Factor.

The Immanuel Factor delivered a boatload of blessings for

Joseph. Protection, prosperity, and promotion came because God was with him. Even his pagan master benefited because God was with Joseph. Joseph's life showed that God makes everything better.

Better, but not easy. Let's read on:

## Joseph Goes to Prison

Now Joseph was well-built and handsome, and after a while his master's wife took notice of Joseph and said, "Come to bed with me!" But he refused. "With me in charge," he told her, "my master does not concern himself with anything in the house; everything he owns he has entrusted to my care. No one is greater in this house than I am. My master has withheld nothing from me except you, because you are his wife. How then could I do such a wicked thing and sin against God?" And though she spoke to Joseph day after day, he refused to go to bed with her or even be with her.

One day he went into the house to attend to his duties, and none of the household servants was inside. She caught him by his cloak and said, "Come to bed with me!" But he left his cloak in her hand and ran out of the house. When she saw that he had left his cloak in her hand and had run out of the house, she called her household servants. "Look," she said to them, "this Hebrew has been brought to us to make sport of us! He came in here to sleep with me, but I screamed. When he heard me scream for help, he left his cloak beside me and ran out of the house." She kept his cloak beside her until his master came home. Then she told him this story: "That Hebrew slave you brought us came to me to make sport of me. But as soon as I screamed for help, he left his cloak beside me and ran out of the house." When his master heard the story his wife told him, saying, "This is how your slave treated me," he burned with anger. Joseph's master took him and put him in prison, the place where the king's prisoners were confined. (Genesis 39:6–20)

When you study it, the quality and quantity of blessing available in the Immanuel Factor is staggering. God is good, and good things flow in His wake. As we will see again and again in the rest of this book, people are said to have experienced success, protection, victory, strength, testimony, fame, prosperity, and promotion because God was with them. It is rather seductive.

But we also live in a world that lives in opposition to God. His will and His ways cut sharply across the ways of the world. The Immanuel Factor guarantees God, but not ease or comfort. It can produce big blessings *and* big trouble. Joseph got both.

Potiphar's wife took a shine to Joseph. She invited him to have sex with her. He had every human reason to acquiesce. Joseph had worked for Potiphar eleven years. He was twenty-eight years old when this temptation came.[1] His sex drive was in high gear. He was away from home. No one would ever know if he accepted the invitation to have sex with Potiphar's wife . . . but God.

So he said no. And he kept saying no until he finally had to physically run from the woman and the sin. God's presence in Joseph's life was so real to him that he would not offend God with any act, no matter how natural and easy such an act would be. The scorned wife quickly cooked up a lie, and her husband had no choice but to act. Joseph was thrown into prison.

Therefore, instead of continuing his climb up, Joseph's career took an ugly turn down. He went from being a slave with increasing freedom and responsibility to being a prisoner.

One could look at these events and conclude that the Immanuel Factor is not such a great deal after all. It only made things better in order to make things worse. Joseph was faithful and true to God, yet where was God now?

### God Goes to Prison

But while Joseph was there in the prison, *the* LORD *was with him*; he showed him kindness and granted him favor in the eyes of the prison warden. So the warden put Joseph in charge of all those held in the prison, and he was made responsible for all that was done there. The warden paid no attention to anything under Joseph's care, because *the* LORD *was with Joseph* and gave him success in whatever he did. (Genesis 39:20–23, emphasis added)

The Lord was with him even while Joseph was in prison. God's presence did not necessarily keep him from trouble, but it went with him through the trouble. And as a result, there was prosperity in the midst of adversity.

Joseph was accused of attempted rape. Scholars tell us that a slave accused of such a crime would have routinely been executed. Yet possibly because of his wife's questionable character, probably because of Joseph's sterling character, and certainly because of the Immanuel Factor, Potiphar did not have Joseph killed. Instead, he sent him to prison. It was a prison for political prisoners that just happened to be located on his property![2]

Soon Joseph had caught the eye of the prison warden, and Joseph was once again in charge. Again he was successful, except this time on a much larger scale. He was not merely running the captain of the guard's household. Now he was running an entire prison. He was getting an advanced course in leadership and management that he would need later. He was hobnobbing with political prisoners and former cabinet members. Joseph had been faithful to God, and God was being faithful to Joseph, just as He had always been before.

And, as we who have read the rest of Genesis know, it was from this prison that God eventually orchestrated the events that placed Joseph in the role of prime minister of Egypt, the greatest nation on earth at that time. Talk about a promotion!

It was as prime minister that Joseph was able to save the world from a horrible famine. It was as prime minister that he also was able to rescue his family, so that the Hebrew nation was spared. (Their bowing down to him was the fulfillment of Joseph's childhood dreams.) And it was as prime minister that he also spared one of his half brothers, Judah, who was in the lineage of the Messiah to come. The Immanuel Factor had allowed God to work things together for good for *many people*, not just Joseph. (See Romans 8:28 and Genesis 50:20.)

In my mind, this makes the ways of God in general, and the Immanuel Factor in particular, extraordinarily powerful and universally superior. Satan has the power to bless his followers. But he lacks the amazing grace and love to go with them through their adversity. And he does not have the astounding wisdom to use adversity to ultimately give them far greater blessings and to position them to be a greater blessing to others. Yeah, God!

## PRINCIPLES OF THE IMMANUEL FACTOR

### 1. The Immanuel Factor can produce blessing.

The Immanuel Factor produced in Joseph's life prosperity (39:2), success (39:3, 23), recognition and testimony (39:3), favor with ungodly authority (39:4, 21), promotion (39:4–5), blessing upon others (39:5), and trust (39:6, 23). It led to protection (39:20) and prime positioning for future promotion (39:1, 20). Not bad, huh?

God is very good, and when God's presence permeates our lives, good things will result. Joseph was not the first to experience blessing from the Immanuel Factor. Others had experienced it prior to this time. Joseph's great-grandfather Abraham lived in such a way that even pagans recognized it and said, "God is with you in everything you do" (Genesis 21:22). Because of Abraham, God promised Isaac that His presence would be with him to bless him (26:3, 24, 28), and He promised the same to Jacob (28:15, 20–21; 31:3).

The patriarchs in general, and Joseph in particular, display the level of blessing available through the Immanuel Factor. From them we learn that if we want to enjoy a life of true prosperity, we must have the manifest presence of God.

### 2. The Immanuel Factor does not make us immune to adversity.

Joseph underwent great adversity. In fact, the Immanuel Factor may actually *produce* adversity. Joseph wouldn't have been thrown into prison if he had succumbed to temptation. And he would have given in if it weren't for the presence of God governing his heart.

The notion that there exists a legitimate form of Christian living that exempts a person from problems and pain is foreign to the Bible. Joseph was an exceptionally good and godly man.

But he was kidnapped, enslaved, slandered against, and falsely imprisoned.

With that said, we should also note that the Immanuel Factor was every bit as powerful—actually, more powerful in adversity than it had been in prosperity. God was not only with Joseph in Canaan but also in Egypt. God was with Joseph as a slave. God was with Joseph in prison. In fact, Joseph experienced more of the manifest presence of God as a slave and prisoner than his forefathers Jacob or Isaac had enjoyed as wealthy ranchers.

The beauty of pure Christianity, as expressed by the Immanuel Factor, is that it not only works when we are seemingly on the way up but also when it appears we are going down. It is in force on the mountaintops, but also flourishes in the valleys. It is every bit as powerful on Monday morning or Friday night as it is on Sunday morning. It is as real in the office or at the kitchen table or in the gym or the classroom as it is in a church sanctuary. God's presence is available in the best of times and the worst of times, on good days and bad, in sunshine and rain, in the prison and in the prime minister's chamber. It also works when life stinks. Just ask John Nelson. . . .

> John Nelson was an early Methodist preacher. Jailed for his faith, he was locked in a cell located below a slaughterhouse. He wrote in his journal, "It stank worse than a pigsty because of the blood and filth that flowed into it from above. But my soul was so filled with the love of God that it was Paradise to me."[3]

God's presence made all the difference.

### 3. The Immanuel Factor helps us reach our destiny.

As a boy God gave Joseph the dream of ruling over others. God's ultimate goal for Joseph was to make him the prime minister of Egypt at a time when he could be used to spare his family and many others from starvation. The route from rancher's son to national ruler was full of obstacles. Kidnapping, slavery, and imprisonment stained the pages of Joseph's life. Yet what man meant for evil in Joseph's life, God turned to good. It was the presence of God all along the way that made it happen. It allowed the ugly pieces of Joseph's life to fit together into a beautiful plan. The evident presence of God permitted Joseph to realize his destiny.

No human fully understands the sovereignty of God. But we can see that the more a person lives for God, the more God works on behalf of that person. Joseph shows us that a life lived in the Immanuel Factor allows God's sovereignty to direct us to our destiny.

### EXPERIENCING IMMANUEL IN A DEATH CAMP

Because of their willingness to hide Jews from the Nazis, the Ten Boom family was sent to the notorious Ravensbruck Concentration Camp, where Corrie and her sister Betsie managed to stay together. Here they experienced not only the depths of man's inhumanity to man but also the power of the Immanuel Factor. Corrie's stories of God's miraculous provision in prison were eventually made into a popular movie called *The Hiding Place*.

Sadly, Betsie did not survive the brutal rigors and severe deprivations of Ravensbruck. Within two weeks of her beloved sister's death, however, Corrie was miraculously released. Years later she learned that her being let go was the result of a clerical error, and shortly afterward, middle-aged women (Corrie's age) were systemically put to death.

After her release, Corrie said,

> God has plans—not problems—for our lives. Before she died in the concentration camp in Ravensbruck, my sister Betsie said to me, "Corrie, your whole life has been a training for the work you are doing here in prison—and for the work you will do afterward."
>
> Looking back across the years of my life, I can see the working of a divine pattern, which is the way of God with His children. When I was in a prison camp in Holland during the war, I often prayed, "Lord, never let the enemy put me in a German concentration camp." God answered no to that prayer. Yet in the German camp, with all its horror, I found

many prisoners who had never heard of Jesus Christ.

If God had not used my sister Betsie and me to bring them to Him, they would never have heard of Him. Many died, or were killed, but many died with the name of Jesus on their lips. They were well worth all our suffering. Faith is like radar, which sees through the fog—the reality of things at a distance that the human eye cannot see.[4]

## 4. The Immanuel Factor is developed over a period of time.

The Immanuel Factor in the life of Joseph was not a one-time outpouring of the presence of God. Instead, it was an ongoing, ever-deepening reality. The core of this story may only cover a single chapter in the Bible and twenty-three short verses, but it spans thirteen years of his life.

We can be easily sabotaged by a quick-fix, instant-gratification, path-of-least-resistance, want-it-all-now mindset. However, learning to experience God and live out His presence is an intentional, continual effort. It is "a long obedience in the same direction."[5] It is a day-in, day-out, disciplined, delightful development of a familiar friendship. The Immanuel Factor is the product of a determined dialogue with the Divine One. We can experience more of God only as we learn to expand our capacity for God. Enjoying the level of the manifest presence of God that Joseph enjoyed takes decision, concentration, commitment, and time. We must do our part to see our heart for God grow and our capacity for God increase.

Joseph's stubborn and heroic refusal to sin was the direct result of his intimate relationship with God. Yes, he did not want to violate his master's trust. Yes, he did not want to stain himself with wickedness. But I believe the primary reason he did not give in was because he could not hurt God.

I want to be so full of love for God that I will not even conceive of anything that might hurt Him. Such a love for God comes only as a result of having spent much time thinking about and communing with Him. God has to be the magnificent obsession and all-consuming passion of our lives.

## 5. The Immanuel Factor is released through resilient loyalty.

The Immanuel Factor can produce amazing and long-lasting prosperity for those who love God with a loyal heart. God was loyal to bless Joseph because Joseph was loyal to live for God no matter where he was, what happened, or how much it cost.

Joseph was cruelly yanked out of his cushy home life and sold as a slave, yet he would not walk away from God. He was lied about and imprisoned falsely, yet he stayed faithful to God. He was forgotten in prison for many years, yet there is no record of his griping or complaining. He continued to faithfully serve both his earthly masters and his heavenly one. Joseph stubbornly refused to get bitter at God.

Even as God blessed him, Joseph did not relax. He did not think that he had gone far enough—that he already had too much of God. He kept up his walk and maintained his integrity. He rested in God, but refused to coast in his relationship with Him.

He was offered a free pass to indulge his sex drive with a powerful woman, but he would not bite. He was nearly executed and subsequently imprisoned because he refused to sin against God. Through it all he remained faithful.

Everyone would love the blessings of Immanuel, but few have the intense love and loyalty for God that rejects any opportunity that might hurt Him. Don't miss the core of this story in the glitter of the potential blessings of the Immanuel Factor. *God is loyal to those who are loyal to Him.* Joseph experienced such extreme levels of prosperity even in the midst of adversity because he was extremely loyal to God. God was with Joseph because Joseph was with Him.

### Expressions of Resilient Loyalty

◆ *Stay faithful to God,* even when someone else's jealousy lands you in dire circumstances—like Joseph's slavery.

Learn it now. Life is hard. There is not always an immediate correlation between walking with God and living in ease. Yet God goes with us to and through the hard places.

◆ *Be steadfast in the face of temptation.*
    Walking with God does not make us immune to temptation. Even Jesus was tempted (Matthew 4:1–11). Temptation tests our allegiance and priorities. The question is: Who comes first, self or God?

◆ *Remain devoted in spite of false accusation and imprisonment.*
    Life is not fair. There is not always an immediate correlation between obedience and blessing. God will go with you into any adversity if you don't abandon Him. Don't let injustice and adversity keep you from Him.

◆ *Don't forget God after getting a giant promotion.*
    Sometimes the greater test of loyalty is not adversity but prosperity. Joseph might have concluded that he did not need God anymore or that he had been good long enough. Fortunately, he knew better than that.

FINAL THOUGHTS

Because they showed the love of Jesus by hiding Jewish people from the Nazis, the Ten Boom family was sent to the Ravensbruck death camp. As Corrie and Betsie were separated from their beloved father, they spoke these words, "God be with you, Papa."

"And God goes with you, my daughters," he replied.

And He did. They remained faithful to God in spite of the worst conditions imaginable. And He remained faithful to them.[6]

After her release from the death camp, Corrie ten Boom shared with audiences all over the world that she had found from experience that *there is no pit so deep that God's love is not deeper still.*

When we approach God with steadfast loyalty, He goes with us through anything—even the worst adversity.

CHAPTER FOUR:

# Son-Shine
## Concentrated Focus

Y OU HAVE SEEN THEM. They are warm and gracious people. There is a golden glow upon them. Goodness and life emanate from their eyes. Love and joy echo from their smile. They have it. The presence of God is all over them. They are experiencing the Shekinah shine of the Immanuel Factor.

My Dad had it. Even through the last year and a half of his life (when he had terminal cancer in every bone in his upper body) it was as though you were in sunshine when you were around him. He spent time with God every morning, and God shined through him the rest of the day. Even though he was in his eighties, he would always be standing at his greeter spot outside, smiling and waving at every car entering our church parking lot on Sunday mornings. Guests would comment on the man whose smile made them feel accepted and welcome.

The last twenty years of her life my mom had it too. She learned to pray in the presence of God, and it showed. In spite of her many physical pains and limitations, her beautiful blue eyes and amazingly generous spirit radiated the life and love of God to all she met. God's love shone through her and warmed even coldhearted people.

Joyce has it. Her depth of passion for the person of God and ability to sit at His feet explains her beaming face and faith-filled words. Those who get near to her end up closer to God.

Andy has it, especially when he leads musical worship. It is as though a sunbeam has fought its way through the clouds in order to burst out all over his smiling face. He is able to lead us into the presence of God because he is no stranger to it.

Mickey has it. Married to a cocaine addict, she has not had it easy in this life. Yet when Mickey sings in the choir, her severely tested love for God makes it impossible for her to refrain from dancing. But she's not the only one. On the other end of the choir, Kathy is every bit as expressive. A former lesbian, she has now made God the King of her heart. Both are contagious worshipers because the presence of God erupting from them sweeps others along in its wake.

Susan, my assistant, also has it. After working together for six years, I can almost always tell when she has had a good time with the Lord in the morning. That's because He shines all over her face and through her "can do" attitude the rest of the day.

And there are many more. You know some as well. They are the people who in their own unique ways and situations radiate the love and glory of God. They are conduits of the presence of God to everyone with whom they come in contact. They are experiencing a measure of the Immanuel Factor. And you can too! Moses will again lead the way.

## Wanting More

A study of Moses' life is a study of encounters with the glory of God. They were not only the defining moments in his life, but also became the distinctive aspects of his personality.

One day God's glory ambushed him from a burning bush and called him to deliver a nation. Another time God appeared to him in a cloud of fiery, thundering glory and gave Moses two tablets of stone that were to become the guidelines for a great nation. Later on God protected Moses by placing him in the crevasse of a boulder. Then God passed by Moses in such an overwhelming display of glory that it would have been fatal if he hadn't been protected by the rock.

Yet these divine encounters were not sufficient for either God or Moses. God seekers always want *more* of God, and God continually desires to pour out more of himself on us.

One of the greatest hindrances to experiencing the Immanuel Factor is our own off-track sense of satisfaction. When it comes to God we are content much too easily with far too little. The many good gifts from God can quickly replace our hunger for His presence.

In contrast to us, Moses had a God-capacity foundational to experiencing God's glorious sufficiency. Even though he had recently finished a forty-day fast in the presence of God, Moses jumped at his opportunity when God called him to come away for more. So he spent forty *more* days fasting.

> Moses was there with the LORD forty days and forty nights without eating bread or drinking water. And he wrote on the tablets the words of the covenant—the Ten Commandments. (Exodus 34:28)

What intense passion for God and concentration on Him! Moses not only did without food, he also did without water. God was literally his food and drink. This is the most extreme fast ever recorded in the Bible, or anywhere else, for that matter.

## MOSES THE MOONIE

> When Moses came down from Mount Sinai with the two tablets of the Testimony in his hands, he was not aware that his face was radiant because he had spoken with the LORD. (Exodus 34:29)

Moses had been with the Lord, and it showed all over his face. Moses had the glow of God on his life. He didn't realize that he had absorbed some of God's glory and was reflecting it from his countenance. In a real sense, Moses' glow was not unlike a man with a sunburn. But in this case it was "Sonburn."

The glow of God on Moses' face was not a self-generated shine. His glow was actually an *after*glow from being in the presence of God. The radiant glory of God was the source of the original shine, and what lingered on Moses' face was merely a reflection of that. So in a sense Moses was a moon to God's sun. He had no light of his own; he merely reflected that which came from God—hence the new handle, Moses the Moonie.

As he spent time in His presence Moses' face reflected God's glory by an evident and obvious shine. "When Aaron and all the Israelites saw Moses, his face was radiant, and they were afraid to come near him" (Exodus 34:30).

There are some Christians who get confused and assume that the mark of God on their lives is the way they dress, the length of their hair, or the big black Bible they carry. Others view it as a cross around their neck, the WWJD bracelet on their wrist, or the Honk-if-you-love-Jesus bumper sticker on their car.

For Moses, the sign of God in his life was the shine of God on his face. Unfortunately, though, the glory faded away when he left God's glorious presence. So Moses covered his face with a veil.

> When Moses finished speaking to them, he put a veil over his face. But whenever he entered the Lord's presence to speak with him, he removed the veil until he came out. And when he came out and told the Israelites what he had been commanded, they saw that his face was radiant. Then Moses would put the veil back over his face until he went in to speak with the LORD. (Exodus 34:33–35)

## PRINCIPLES OF THE IMMANUEL FACTOR

### 1. The Immanuel Factor may radiate on our faces.

Moses is not the only one to have a "Sonburn." Stephen, "the preachin' deacon," had one when he preached his final message before being martyred. Luke wrote,

> All who were sitting in the Sanhedrin looked intently at Stephen, and they saw that his face was like the face of an angel. (Acts 6:15)

John Wesley was a great church leader in his time as well as the founder of the Methodist church. He was the father of the great spiritual awakening that shook England and America with revival in the 1700s. And he had the glow. One of his many biographers noted,

He was a man who sought to keep the glow of God in his life shining at such a white heat that others should recognize it and be led to seek the same transforming power.[1]

Charles Spurgeon was the most influential preaching pastor of his generation. He ministered in London, England, in the 1800s. He led one of the first mega-churches with over five thousand members. On occasion he preached to crowds of over twenty thousand, which was unheard of in his day. His biographer made this observation about his congregation:

While they were worshipping with him the glory of the Lord shone round about them, and this has never been to the same extent their experience in listening to any other man.[2]

You don't have to be a great preacher to shine. Connie and Marilyn are both widows. They meet daily for an hour of prayer, sometimes in person but often over the phone. And it shows on their faces, giving them a wonderful godly beauty. As Titus 2:3–5 women, they lead a small group for "older women" who selflessly and joyfully model dedicated and delightful godliness to younger women in the congregation. I have never been around Connie or Marilyn without feeling honored, loved, encouraged, and lifted. I can tell that they really pray for me, and when I am with them I sense the Holy Spirit hovering close by.

## 2. The Immanuel Factor is more about total transformation than mere facial radiation.

In the book of Second Corinthians Paul mentions Moses' second forty-day experience with God's glory. Paul explains that as Moses reflected the glory of God under the old covenant, the followers of Jesus should radiate the glory of God under the new covenant. He tells them that the glory radiating in and through them is *superior* to the shine of Moses, because it involves total transformation of their character, not merely a shine upon their face that quickly fades.

Since the coming of Jesus, you and I can experience the shine of God as the sign of God in, on, and with us. However, unlike Moses' glow, ours need not fade over time. In fact, it can grow. Paul writes,

> Now the Lord is the Spirit, and where the Spirit of the Lord is, there is freedom. And we, who with unveiled faces all reflect the Lord's glory, are being transformed into his likeness with ever-increasing glory, which comes from the Lord, who is the Spirit. (2 Corinthians 3:17–18)

The goal for Christians is to have our character changed into the personality of Jesus. When I started out with Jesus, I had a contagious love for Him. But I also had many serious flaws in my character. I still have a long way to go, but by the grace of God my character is much more like Jesus than it used to be. A long time ago I came to a challenging realization: I could never get away from *me*. I could get away from everyone else, but I could never get away from me. Therefore, I had better be able to respect the person I have become. I have found that I feel best about the person I am when I spend the most time in the presence of the Person I most want to emulate: Jesus. The more time I spend getting alone with God, the more I come away being like His Son.

This not only worked for Moses and works for me, it also works for all who long to remain in His presence and reflect His glory. Debbie and her husband, Rick, work long hours, but they are still prayer warriors and have such an obvious Son-shine. Laurie is a wife and mother, but you can always tell that she has been with the Lord. The same is true of Kristy. Tina, a wife and mother, works two demanding jobs. But her smile is a sure sign that she spends time focused on Jesus.

Recently a group of teenagers shared with me how they were drawn to Christ. One after another told of having a Christian friend whose obvious love for God, genuine smile, and transformed character attracted them. So they decided to check out Christianity for themselves. What a testimony! What they noticed in their Christian friend was the joy, the peace, the love, and the power to do the right thing that is only possible through knowing Jesus. The divinely renovated personality of their Christian friend made them thirsty to meet the One who had produced such a wonderful person.

3. **The Immanuel Factor is released by a concentrated focus on God.**

Moses got away for an extended period of time, alone, and without food, to give his total concentration to God. He got so close to God that God's presence literally radiated from his face.

I live in Ohio. You can't get sunburned in Ohio in the winter, but you sure can in the summer. The sun is the same in January as it is in July, but the earth is further away and at a different angle to the sun. So its rays are not received at the same level of intensity.

Many people would like to radiate a godly glow, but it won't happen if we are not close enough to God and don't spend enough time in His presence. It won't happen if other things crowd Him out or our intensity in seeking Him is weak.

### Elements of Concentrated Focus in the Presence of God

#### BE OPEN

Moses wore a veil to hide his face. We tend to hide behind veils as well. Yet transformation cannot take place until the veil is removed and we look into God's face with openness. This means that we come to God in absolute honesty, genuine integrity, and complete vulnerability. We must bring the real "us" to meet with the real God.

We will never get a transforming look at God until we give God a transparent look at us. No Pharisee had the glow of God. They couldn't, because their religion was all outward show instead of inward reality.

As a pastor I especially enjoy ministering to teenagers and young adults. During the school year between forty and sixty high school students come to our home each week to meet with God and study His Word. One of our "rules" is that you must be willing to "let God speak to you." Many are, and He does.

Some of them truly glow with God. Even though many of the shining ones are very young in the faith, they are all open in face. They make up for limited years through unlimited access. They don't hide or play games with God. They are honest, often painfully and shockingly so. They admit struggles, acknowledge sin, and come to God without pretense. They come without a veil. They come in hungry desperation and bald openness. And they come away with a beautiful "Sonburn."

### FIND SOLITUDE

The sad reality is that most of us are too busy; our lives are too crowded and cluttered to experience true transformation from the presence of God. Most of us have lives filled with too much activity, too much noise, and too many people, leaving us with little time left for spending time with God.

Moses experienced the Immanuel Factor because he spent quality and quantity time focused on the presence of God. He gazed at the fire of God's presence and glowed as a result. If we want what he had, we must do what he did.

Transformation comes, in part, from shutting ourselves away from people so we can shut ourselves away with God. It is escaping the sound of human voices so we can hear the voice of God. It means a voluntary abstinence from our normal patterns of activity and interaction with people for a time in order to rediscover that our strength, well-being, and transformation come from God alone.

Henri Nouwen notes, "Without solitude it is virtually impossible to lead a spiritual life."[3] Why is this so? Because in worshipful solitude we are freed from our bondage to clatter, clutter, and crowds. Then we can hear, feel, touch, taste, and know God. In a healthy detachment from the world we find a special attachment to God.

Jesus, our example, got up early in the morning so He could start His day in prayer (Mark 1:35). If the Son of God needed worshipful solitude, how much more do you and I?

I find daily solitude by either spending time with God before everyone else in my house is up or after they go to bed. One day a week I love to go to a park and sit there with God for anywhere from a half-hour to an hour. Every month or so I enjoy spending a morning alone with God at my sister-in-law's house, when she and her husband are at work. Then once a year I try to spend a few days alone with God in a hotel. During these sweet times of solitude I not only renew and deepen my connection with God, but I also increase my capacity for God and His presence.

Maybe you can't get away for a day or a morning at a time. Finding even an hour alone with God seems impossible. Let me encourage you to make the most of the time you do get to spend with God. Turning off the TV, getting up an hour early, and spending time with God over your lunch break are all ways busy people connect with God.

### KEEP COMING BACK

Maybe you started reading this book because you were looking for a quick fix, an instant spiritual face-lift, some immediate "heart surgery." Sorry. There is no such thing as instant spiritual transformation. It is an ongoing process of ever-increasing glory. Our character is transformed little by little, a bit at a time.

Some of the most Christlike, beautiful, glowing people I know are also some of the oldest I know in terms of age. But at the same time many of the ungodliest people I have met, with the most unattractive personalities, are also elderly. Why the extremes? The seniors who are the most like Jesus have been spending quality time with Him daily *for a long time.* They have been "transformed into his likeness with ever-increasing glory" (2 Corinthians 3:18) over a period of years—decades actually. As for the others, the longer they have avoided His presence the more unlike Him they have become.

The simple rule of human nature is that we tend to take on the characteristics and attitudes of the people we are around most frequently. If we hope to reflect the personality and mindset of Jesus we must spend time with Him.

Moses glowed with God after being with God. He spent forty days focused solely on God. That's sixteen waking hours a day, 112 hours a week, for six weeks, with God. That's quality and *quantity* time with God.

Make no mistake about it. We will not be able to experience the Immanuel Factor if we do not experience Immanuel. And we won't experience Immanuel if we don't invest quantity and quality time focused on Him, lost in His presence. Five minutes a day won't keep the devil away, and it won't produce true lasting transformation either.

## FAST FROM FOOD IN ORDER TO FEAST ON GOD

Fasting is a voluntary exercise of discipline that aids our ability to focus on God. Saying no to food enables us to concentrate on God more clearly and hear His voice more accurately. It brings us closer to Him so we can be changed into His image.

In recent years the Western church has rediscovered the spiritual discipline of fasting. From one meal a day to one day a week, many Christians have happily learned to say no to food in order to say yes to a deeper encounter with God.

Fasting, as used in the Bible, means "self-denial." Fasting is choosing not to partake of food because spiritual hunger is so deep, determination in intercession is so intense, or spiritual warfare is so demanding that you temporarily set aside even fleshly needs to give yourself more wholly to prayer. A normal fast involves abstaining from all food, but not from water (see Matthew 4:2). Typically, fasting went for one complete twenty-four-hour period, from one sundown to the next sundown. The early church fasted two days every week, Wednesday and Friday. Other biblical fasts went from three to forty days. Both individual and corporate fasts are mentioned in the Scriptures. Fasting may also include skipping a meal consistently or abstaining from certain foods or activities.[4]

Fasting is not a new idea. Jesus advocated proper fasting. He taught that after He, the heavenly Bridegroom, ascended to heaven, fasting was to become a regular discipline in the life of His disciples:

> Jesus answered, "How can the guests of the bridegroom mourn while he is with them? The time will come when the

bridegroom will be taken from them; then they will fast" (Matthew 9:15).

At this point you are probably in one camp or another on fasting. The thought of going a whole day without food is overwhelming to some of you. Because of the way you grew up, it seems unnatural and unhealthy. On the other hand, some of us overzealous types are ready to sign up for the forty-day fast right now. Wisdom lies in the middle.

If you have never skipped a meal to feast on God, start there. I suggest that you develop your capacity to fast just as you develop any other muscle. Start with one meal. Then try one day. Then attempt a three-day fast. Then maybe go for a week. I have found no one who fasted for more than a week who did not feel "called" to it. Forty days is a long time. It's almost six weeks.

Maybe health reasons limit your ability to fast from food altogether. If so, then try fasting from certain foods as Daniel did (Daniel 1), or from certain activities. Evelyn Christensen, author of the bestselling book *When Women Pray*, fasts from sleep in order to give herself more completely to God in prayer.

Let me also say very clearly: Don't fast more than a day or two without drinking fluids. Otherwise, you will become dangerously dehydrated and could do serious damage to your liver and kidneys.

But the point of this chapter is not to tell you everything you need to know about fasting. There are plenty of excellent books that teach all the ins and outs of fasting. The point of this chapter is to see what happened as a result of Moses' effort to concentrate his focus on God.

Let me encourage you to take the initiative to make some divine appointments with God. Fill out the chart below. You will be very glad you did.

This week my daily time with God will be: _____.
I hope to spend some extra special time with God on _____ (date), from _____ to _____ (time).

CHAPTER FIVE:

# No Fear
## Courageous Obedience

TWENTY-SIX-YEAR-OLD ASHLEY SMITH had only lived in her apartment two days. She got out of the car and walked to the door. Fear flowed down her spine like ice water as a man came up behind her, stuck a gun to her head, and forced her inside.

Fear increased when she realized that she was the hostage of accused rapist Brian Nichols. Days earlier Nichols had gone on a bloody killing spree, leaving four people dead as he escaped from an Atlanta courthouse. Nichols, running from police, just happened to show up at her door.

Smith, a young widow, was newly involved in a Celebrate Recovery group at a local church, seeking the help of God to overcome her battle with drug and alcohol addiction. Fearing rape and murder, Smith silently sought God for the supernatural courage to talk to Nichols through the night.

At one point he let her read her Bible. Then he even let her read to him a section of a Christian book about how the purpose of life is to serve others. She told him that he needed to turn himself in and stop hurting people. He needed to go to prison and share the Word of God with the other prisoners.

The next day, as Ashley calmly served him pancakes, murderer-rapist Brian Nichols looked at her and said he believed she was an angel sent from God. He was lost and needed her to tell him to stop hurting people.

Eventually, he allowed her to leave the apartment. Shortly after, he surrendered to the police.

As it was recorded in newspapers across America, Ashley Smith found that God gave her a supernatural courage to overcome her fear and minister in a very dangerous and unusual way. She said, "I believe God brought him to my door so he would not hurt anyone else."[1]

## What Are You Afraid Of?

What is your greatest fear? One recent survey said 41 percent of us are most afraid of snakes; 26 percent are most afraid of public speaking; 19 percent, high, open spaces; 16 percent, mice; 16 percent, flying on a plane; and 11 percent, spiders and insects. Another team of researchers discovered financial problems, deep water, sickness, death, loneliness, dogs, darkness, elevators, and escalators to be top human fears. We could add to this list the fear of losing a job, old age, something negative happening to our children, being robbed, being hurt physically by another, natural disasters, terrorism, or war. I often struggle with fears surrounding the uncertainty of the future. And my biggest fear is the fear of failure.

Have you ever had that scared-to-death, paralyzed-with-panic, dead-with-dread, "I am in way over my head" or "I don't think I can do this" feeling? I have, more often than I care to admit. I felt it my first day in high school; I also had it when I went on my first real date, when I wrestled in the state tournament, and my first day of college. I had a slight flare-up of it on the beautiful day when I stood in a little church in rural Pennsylvania and watched Cathy, my wife, come down the aisle in a lovely white dress. I felt it as I planned for the first worship service of the brand new church we had birthed. And it nearly overwhelmed me three different times as I stood in the hospital beside Cathy's bed, holding each of my newborn sons in my arms for the first time.

When we confront new responsibilities and greater challenges, it is common to be hit with insecurity, anxiety, and fear. Sometimes it pounds us in waves, relentlessly sweeping over us.

At other times the panic-plagued emotions and terrifying thoughts simmer and boil from within. Our fears create a deep vacuum in our stomach that sucks the life, peace, and joy from our lives.

The focus of our Immanuel Factor quest now shifts from Moses to his successor, Joshua. If anyone wrestled with insecurity, uncertainty, and anxiety in the face of a huge new responsibility, it was Joshua. Yet he became a victorious follower of God. Let's see how it happened.

## All Shook Up

The legendary leader Moses had passed away. Before he died, he knighted a younger man, his lieutenant Joshua, to serve as his successor and head up the infant Hebrew nation. This riotous rabble of ex-slaves had wandered around the desert wilderness for forty years, plagued primarily by their own doubt and rebellion. Leading them was like herding spiders. Moses had only succeeded because of the manifest presence of God. Now it all fell on Joshua's shoulders, plus much more.

They were camped on the edge of the Promised Land, grieving the death of their renowned leader, Moses. The next task was to somehow cross the Jordan River and defeat the wicked pagan peoples who occupied the land. Conquering the Promised Land would serve a dual purpose. The barbaric peoples would be judged for their perversion and violence, and the people of God would be given the land God had promised hundreds of years earlier. It was up to Joshua to be the point man for this overwhelming responsibility.

As he faced this massive assignment Joshua wrestled with the expected sense of awful anxiety and disabling dread. Joshua was in way over his head, and he was rattled by it. I am sure his mind was flooded with questions such as:

*How are we going to do this?*

*What are the odds of our succeeding?*

*Are we up to the task?*

*If Moses had difficulty keeping these people in line, how can I do it?*

*Why me? Why this? Why now?*

Fear, along with its evil twin worry, are two all-too-common cancers that consume the life of many Christians. Dread drains our strength. Out-of-control concerns create confusion and cripple our concentration. Anxiety sabotages our joy and assaults our peace, immobilizing and derailing us.

And it is all so unnecessary.

## God Does Not Sweat

God has many astounding attributes. He is fabulously creative, absolutely infinite, totally dominant, and supremely wise. God is good, gracious, generous, merciful, and faithful. He is not only true, He *is* the truth. He is courageously caring and compassionate. God is ageless and timeless, yet completely contemporary. He knows and understands every little thing about every single thing. He hurts, grieves, laughs, and weeps. But He never, ever, sweats.

Even though Joshua was all shook up, God was not rattled. His tiny nation of followers stood on the brink of possible drowning, defeat, or annihilation. No sweat. God had the matter in hand, and He had Joshua in mind. God knew all about Joshua's anxiety. And He had the answer.

> After the death of Moses the servant of the LORD, the LORD said to Joshua son of Nun, Moses' aide: "Moses my servant is dead. Now then, you and all these people, get ready to cross the Jordan River into the land I am about to give to them—to the Israelites. I will give you every place where you set your foot, as I promised Moses. Your territory will extend from the desert to Lebanon, and from the great river, the Euphrates—all the Hittite country—to the Great Sea on the west. No one will be able to stand up against you all the days of your life. As I was with Moses, so *I will be with you*; I will never leave you nor forsake you" (Joshua 1:1–5, emphasis added).

## PRINCIPLES OF THE IMMANUEL FACTOR

### 1. God's presence is the prescription for victory over fear.

In a few sentences, God told Joshua exactly what he needed to hear. He addressed Joshua's deepest fears and offered the promise that can dwarf any fear: "As I was with Moses, so I will be with you." God's presence is the prescription for overcoming panic. Those had to have been the sweetest words Joshua had ever heard. It was the presence of God that had made Moses effective, and it would be the presence of God that would see Joshua through his leadership challenges also.

#### SOMEONE BIGGER AND STRONGER

Sometimes the presence of someone bigger and stronger erases our fears. My oldest son has always had a difficult time going to sleep. When he was a toddler, I had to be present with him in his room before he would go to sleep. I still remember his little routine. After he had been in bed several minutes, I'd hear him rustle around. Then his small wide-eyed face would peep up over the side of his crib. He would scan the room until he saw me sitting quietly in the chair reading. Then he'd smile, sigh, lie down, go immediately to sleep, and start to snore.

One night after he had been in bed a few minutes, I got an idea. I hid just out of sight in order to see what he'd do—big mistake! He popped his head up, looked frantically around, and concluded that I was not present. His tiny face puckered up, he opened his mouth, and then he . . . *screamed*! Boy, did he scream.

For him, the absence of Dad released the presence of fear. Seeing the terror in his little face made me feel awful. Feebly trying to explain my idea to his mom made me feel worse.

### 2. God's presence whips wimps into warriors.

Years after Joshua was gone, a man named Gideon experienced the need for the Immanuel Factor. As happened repeatedly after the days of Joshua, Israel had wandered from following God, so God removed His hand of protection on the nation.

As a result, desert raiders could swoop in on their camels and steal all of their valuables, livestock, and crops. Most of the people of Israel cowered in constant fear, some fleeing to live in caves and dens.

So it was with Gideon. He was hiding away, threshing grain in a winepress. Grain was usually threshed on the top of a hill so the wind could blow away the chaff. But the situation was so desperate he had to thresh it down in a valley, hiding down low in a winepress in order not to be seen by the Midianites. Instead of the wind automatically taking care of separating the chaff from the grain, Gideon had to throw it into the air and hope a bit of the chaff would blow away. No doubt such a position of weakness frustrated him greatly. But one day, out of nowhere, a messenger from God suddenly appeared to him.

> When the angel of the LORD appeared to Gideon, he said, "The LORD is with you, mighty warrior" (Judges 6:12).

Notice that the messenger called Gideon a "mighty warrior." Just picture the irony of this bizarre event. A grown man was hiding in a winepress when God's angel appeared and called him "mighty warrior." What was God doing? Bible commentators are divided at this point. Some say Gideon had a reputation as a warrior among the upper class of Israel.[2] Others say this is another example of God's great sense of humor.[3] Still others feel that this is a prophetic word describing Gideon's destiny.

I think it is all three. God does have a wonderful sense of humor. Also, later events would indicate that Gideon did indeed have a background in battle, but he had not yet fulfilled this part of his destiny.

The trouble was, up until this point, Gideon was a man full of fear. His eyes were on himself, and he knew that he was insufficient. So he questioned God's call to lead. "But Lord," Gideon asked, "how can I save Israel? My clan is the weakest in Manasseh, and I am the least in my family" (Judges 6:15).

God's answer was immediate and clear. "'You can rescue Israel because I am going to help you! Defeating the Midianites will be as easy as beating up one man'" (Judges 6:16 CEV).

God's message was simple: If Gideon would go into battle, God would go with him. The rest of the story is a wonderful example of God's ironic sense of humor and irrefutable power.

God ordered the previously cowardly Gideon to whittle a potential army of thirty-two thousand down to a mere three hundred. To us, this sounds like a crazy strategy. Yet these three hundred men, with the manifest presence of God, did what thirty-two thousand had been unable to do without it. They fearlessly and totally routed their enemies and delivered their land from the oppressors.

God's presence transformed a wimp into a warrior. It changed cowardice into confidence and courage. It was the determining factor. It was the enabling strength. It was the provision for victory.

## 3. God's presence guarantees our peace.

Another favorite story from the Old Testament involves the prophet Elisha as he calmly drove the enemy, the king of Aram, to distraction. Elisha was able to tell the king of Israel everything his enemy, the king of Aram, planned to do. The king of Aram couldn't defeat the Israelites because they already knew his plans.

The king of Aram got so upset that he sent an entire army to capture Elisha, who was staying in a town called Dothan. Elisha's assistant got up in the morning to find the city surrounded with Aram's army. He and Elisha seemingly had no way to escape. The servant ran up to Elisha and in effect frantically cried, "We're surrounded, we're surrounded; what shall we do, what shall we do?"

To this Elisha calmly replied, "Don't be afraid. . . . Those who are with us are more than those who are with them" (2 Kings 6:16). Then we read that Elisha prayed something like this: "God, open this poor guy's eyes so he can see things from your point of view."

And the servant's eyes were opened. He immediately saw that God's larger army of angels surrounded Aram's large army of men. The point is: When God's people are fulfilling God's will they don't need to be afraid. God's presence gives us protection.

Of course, there are times when God has a higher purpose in mind. Many in the early church were martyred. Missionaries through the ages have sometimes lost their lives sharing the Gospel. Yet God's presence was always with them, giving them a peace that truly surpassed all human understanding.

## 4. God goes into the fire.

Isaiah was a prophet who offered prophetic words of encouragement to the faithful followers of God. One of Isaiah's strong words of encouragement quenches fear.

> "Fear not, for I have redeemed you; I have called you by your name; you are Mine. When you pass through the waters, *I will be with you*; and through the rivers, they shall not overflow you. When you walk through the fire, you shall not be burned, nor shall the flame scorch you. For I am the LORD your God" (Isaiah 43:1–3 NKJV, emphasis added).

The statement "When you walk through the fire, you shall not be burned, nor shall the flame scorch you" is especially interesting. There were three Israelites who did face fire for their faith. Do you remember their names? Yes, Shadrach, Meshach, and Abednego. They were to be executed in a furnace of fire because they had refused to worship an image of King Nebuchadnezzar.

Yet when the king looked into the furnace he was astounded to find them amazingly immune to the flames. Nebuchadnezzar was so outraged by their boldness that he had the furnace cranked up seven times hotter than usual. It was so hot that the heat killed the soldiers standing guard nearby.

When the king looked in again, he not only saw the three Hebrew men unburned, but he saw a fourth person in the fire with them. He said, "'The fourth looks like a son of the gods'" (Daniel 3:25). He was close. The fourth was not "a son of the gods," but *the Son of God*. They were not alone—the preincarnate Jesus was with them in the fire.

Because of the Immanuel Factor, those three men didn't only escape death, they escaped all the effects of the fire—their robes weren't scorched, not one hair was singed, and they didn't even smell like smoke! On top of all that, King Nebuchadnezzar was so impressed by what God had done on their behalf that he decreed that no one in his land was permitted to say a word against the God of Shadrach, Meshach, and Abednego. Then for good measure he gave them all a promotion! (See Daniel 3:1–30 for full details.) The presence of God secured these men's protection, enabled their promotion, and expanded God's testimony within the pagan land of Babylon. Never underestimate the power of Immanuel!

Maybe you are currently facing a "fire." The "heat" of the situation appears to be all-consuming. The "flames" are more than you can bear. Have no fear. God is there. When He allows His children to face the fire, He goes through it with them.

Tammy has been in the fire. First, she discovered that her husband was involved in a gay relationship. When confronted about it, he asked for a divorce. Then her daughter plunged into a suicidal depression. Yet Tammy knew God was with her. He came in the form of her church family. Some helped her and her girls to find a place to live. Others aided them when they moved. Several purchased furniture and household goods to get them started. A few counseled her daughter out of her depression and led her to Christ. Another walked Tammy through the flames of her sudden financial nightmare and overwhelming legal proceedings. All told, more than twenty-five Christian friends helped Tammy and her girls. Make no mistake, it *was* a fire. But God was with her all the way.

## 5. God's presence surrounds us when we obey anyway.

Going back to the book of Joshua, we discover that the Immanuel Factor is conditional. The level of God's presence with Joshua was determined by the extent of his obedience to God.

"Be strong and very courageous. Be careful to obey all the law my servant Moses gave you; do not turn from it to the right or to the left, that you may be successful wherever you go. Do not let this Book of the Law depart from your mouth; meditate on it day and night, so that you may be careful to do everything written in it. Then you will be prosperous and successful. Have I not commanded you? Be strong and courageous. Do not be terrified; do not be discouraged, for the LORD your God will be with you wherever you go" (Joshua 1:7–9).

Joshua's success was conditional: He had to have God's presence. And God's presence was dependent upon Joshua's obedience. In other words, God promised to bless him and be with him *as long as* Joshua would get out of his comfort zone and obey God's instructions.

We know that God's abiding presence is promised to His children; therefore, He will never leave us or forsake us. Yet we can increase the amount of God's manifest presence in our lives by increasing our level of obedience.

### THE COURAGE TO FORGIVE

As I write this, I just arrived home from church where an evangelist named Ken Freeman shared his testimony. This man has an unusual anointing of the manifest presence of God on his speaking ministry. Tonight, as has happened all week, dozens of people responded to his invitation to be saved.

His story is riveting. Abandoned at the age of four by his father, he was raised by his alcoholic mother. In drunken rages she would often beat him and his sister. She would tell Ken that he was a mistake, unwanted, and unloved. She even went so far as to say he should be killed.

He had nine stepfathers over the course of his childhood. He was abused both physically and sexually, abandoned for days at a time, and threatened with a butcher knife. He attended twenty-five different schools and moved out on his own at the age of fourteen. He slept in cars, yards, and alleys. On occasion he was taken in by a friend.

When he was a teenager, a friend invited him to attend a revival service at a church. While at that service God's love overwhelmed Ken, and he was saved. As a new Christian he felt the call of God into the ministry. Yet he wrestled with victory over sin, lacking spiritual power in his life. A friend told him, "You'll never know the power of the presence of God until you forgive your parents."

As you can imagine, Ken hated his parents and wanted them dead. Extending forgiveness to them was beyond his imagination. But *he obeyed anyway*. Ken called them up and asked them to forgive him for hating them. As a result of his courageous obedience, his father was saved and Ken's own heart was set free. Then his ministry could take off as the powerful anointing of God's presence empowered him.

## God Is in the River

On the heels of God's word of encouragement and instruction came Joshua's first opportunities to obey. These would be high risk/high reward, big faith/no-room-for-fear acts of obedience.

First, he was commanded to lead the people through the Jordan River by faith. The strategy was crazy. The people were to follow the priests into the raging river. The priests carried the ark of the covenant, symbolizing the presence of God. They had to have the faith that God would hold back the waters so they could cross. The water was fast and the current impassable without His intervention. Obedience would be perilous at best, deadly at worst. If God did not accompany them and work a miracle, people would die and Joshua's authority would be shot.

Yet Joshua's faith was greater than his fear, and he obeyed anyway. God came through.

> Now the Jordan is at flood stage all during harvest. Yet as soon as the priests who carried the ark reached the Jordan and their feet touched the water's edge, the water from upstream stopped flowing. It piled up in a heap a great distance away, at a town called Adam in the vicinity of Zarethan, while the water flowing down to the Sea of the Arabah

(the Salt Sea) was completely cut off. So the people crossed over opposite Jericho. (Joshua 3:15–16)

Just as God had led the people through the Red Sea with Moses, now He led the people through the Jordan River with Joshua. Miraculously, the water stood still until nearly a million people passed through under Moses' guidance. When Joshua obeyed, God also granted him a miracle of safe passage for everyone.

God's manifest presence was not apparent when they were on the banks. It appeared when they left the banks and stepped out into the rushing water. God was *in* the river, not on the side. His presence was not revealed until they got their feet wet. If they had refused to obey and stayed on the side, they would have lost the amazing joy they must have experienced when they stepped into the rushing water and found Him to be there with them.

### GOD KNOCKS DOWN THE WALLS

But the testing of Joshua's obedience was not complete when they crossed the Jordan. Joshua's next assignment was to begin to capture the land, city-state by city-state. Ironically, the first point of attack was the best-defended city in the world. Jericho had walls thick enough to drive a chariot on top. Their defenses had never been threatened and were considered to be completely impregnable.

Not only did Joshua have to take this city, he had to do it without attacking it. God's command was to march the entire Israelite army around the city for six days in a row. On the seventh day, they were to walk around it seven times, blowing trumpets and shouting the victory—another seemingly absurd strategy.

Joshua put aside his fear and obeyed anyway. He rallied the army to march around the walls six days in a row. I can imagine how the warriors on the walls of Jericho jeered at them for such strange behavior. Walking around the walls was especially risky because it left them open to being shot by enemy archers on the walls. But they obeyed God anyway, and they were kept safe.

On the seventh day, they marched around seven times, as commanded, and then blew their trumpets. By faith they shouted the victory. And to their delight it worked. In response to their fulfilling every command given by God, the presence of Immanuel worked a mighty miracle.

> When the trumpets sounded, the people shouted, and at the sound of the trumpet, when the people gave a loud shout, the wall collapsed; so every man charged straight in, and they took the city. (Joshua 6:20)

The thick, strong, and seemingly invincible walls fell inward, destroying the city's inhabitants and leaving Joshua's men unharmed. When Joshua obeyed, even when it made no sense, God blessed him with success through a truly incredible miracle. The victory they had claimed by faith became a reality.

### Courageous Obedience Must Become a Lifestyle

The rest of his life Joshua found the promises he had received to hold true. He was wise enough to make courageous obedience a lifestyle, not merely a one-time event. As long as he continued to obey God, His manifest presence chased away Joshua's fears and gave him great success.

> So the LORD was with Joshua, and his fame spread throughout the land. (Joshua 6:27)

That's the challenge, isn't it? Obeying when you don't feel like it, doing right when it's not easy, and following God when no one is applauding.

I think that the longer we courageously obey God, the more our capacity to experience and manifest God grows. Let me challenge you to a 24/7, every-day-of-the-year lifestyle that fearlessly follows God—no matter what.

I took an IQ (intelligence quotient) test in school that measured aspects of my intelligence. It placed a numeric score on my level of intelligence compared to the rest of the population.

Today, high school juniors and seniors are awarded scholarships to college based proportionately on the results of the ACT (American College Testing) and SAT (Scholastic Aptitude Test) scores. The higher the test scores, the bigger the scholarship.

A more important test for us as Christians would be our OQ (obedience quotient), measuring our obedience aptitude and level. God awards His manifest presence proportionately, based on our willingness to obey Him regardless of the risks. The higher our OQ score the greater the level of the manifest presence of God in our lives. Here are some questions to help you determine your current OQ.

- ◆ What is it God has told you *not* to do, but you continue to do anyway?
- ◆ What is it that God has told you *to do*, but you have put off doing because it is uncomfortable?
- ◆ Where have you let fear keep you from obeying?
- ◆ Will you obey God even when it is risky?

### How to Live a Life of Courageous Obedience

1. Tell God that you are willing to do anything He tells you to do, go anywhere He wants you to go, and be anything He asks you to be.
2. Be sure that what you think God is telling you to do is confirmed by His Word.
3. Once that is settled, don't debate, don't doubt, and don't delay. Obey anyway.

CHAPTER SIX:

# God Is Gone
## His Aversion to Arrogance

THE JIM AND TAMMY FAYE STORY became one of the ugliest scandals to ever hit American Christianity. In 1967, televangelist Jim Bakker and his wife, Tammy Faye, started *The PTL Club*. (PTL is an acronym for Praise the Lord and People That Love). *The PTL Club* became one of the most popular televised ministries of its time. In 1984, their ministry added Heritage USA, a Christian theme park. The way the Bakkers told it, prosperity was a gift from God. They saw their army of followers and immense personal fortunes as proof of their claim. Everything around them did seem blessed . . . until a series of scandals broke in 1987.

Jim was caught funneling $265,000 in hush money to church secretary Jessica Hahn, to cover up their adulterous relationship. Newspaper reporters began to investigate the organization and discovered serious financial wrongdoings; they revealed that the Bakkers and their empire had blown through $158 million of their ministry's donations. Jim Bakker resigned from his position at PTL in the wake of the scandal and was put on trial. Subsequently convicted of fraud and conspiring to commit fraud, he was sentenced to forty-five years in prison and given a $500,000 fine. He served almost five years in prison before being paroled for good behavior.

Jim admitted squandering church donations on luxury cars and six mansions. When he finally got caught, there were forty-seven separate bank accounts in his name. After wasting money on every conceivable normal luxury, the Bakkers had obviously brainstormed some truly frivolous expenditures, like $100 in cinnamon buns just to imbue their hotel suite with the fresh-baked smell, a doghouse equipped with air-conditioning (which proved to be too noisy for their dog to sleep in), and $60,000 in gold-plated bathroom fixtures.

Also convicted and sent to prison was Richard Dortch, senior vice-president of PTL and associate pastor of Heritage Village Church. Dortch later said, "Pride, arrogance, and secrets led to the PTL scandal. While most people never face temptations on the same scale, the ingredients for seemingly smaller failures are the same." Dortch said the men in PTL's leadership felt they were above accountability. They felt specially called by God and accountable only to Him. He said they didn't plan the scandal; instead, it was the natural result of living for oneself rather than for God.[1]

Looking back on his time in prison, Jim Bakker said, "The first months of prison were devastating. After being in a public ministry every day of your life and then finding yourself with everything gone—not only the material things, but friends and reputation—and facing forty-five years, you wonder, Is God gone too? I began to seek God, but I couldn't find him."[2]

### The Man Who Could Do No Wrong

In his autobiography, *The Man Who Could Do No Wrong*, Charles Blair recounts his sad story of painful regret. As a boy Charles endured fierce times growing up on the wrong side of the tracks, in Oklahoma, during the Great Depression. Deeply ashamed of his family's poverty, he dreamed of accomplishment, applause, and success.

Charles was unusually gifted in ministry. He built one of the largest churches in America in the 1970s. It had a huge radio and TV ministry, and a missionary outreach around the world. Not content with that, blind ambition and an oversized ego led Blair to try to create a massive medical center as well. When banks refused to loan the church the millions of dollars needed for this venture, Blair took the church through the illegal sale of financial securities. A huge amount of money was borrowed from private investors. When the church was slow to repay, more securities were sold and more money borrowed.

To compound the financial problems, construction costs exceeded their projections. Soon the ministry was stuck in no-man's-land—not having the money to finish the medical center and no way to generate any income to repay the debts they had already run up. So bankruptcy proceedings began. Investors were afraid that they would not receive any return on their investments. With the debt continuing to mount, Blair was finally brought to court and charged with fraud.

The case played out in headlines across the country, as he was made the poster child for a man caught in the trap of his own ego and image. A gifted man who allowed himself to become consumed with appearances was now accused of cheating and stealing.

After a long and painful trial, the verdict came back from the jury:

"Guilty."

### The Pain of Regret

King Saul would be able to commiserate with Jim Bakker and Charles Blair. Like them, Saul would have gladly given everything he ever owed to *begin again*. The bleeding bodies of his troops littering the slopes of Mount Gilboa were silent yet elegant memorials of his many mistakes. In his final hours the enemy closed in and his life spun wildly to its inevitable end. Hungry, hunted, hurting, and heartbroken, Saul was haunted by flashbacks of what had been and what could have been. His sons were dead, his army was crushed, and his kingdom was ripped from his grasp—all the result of his poor choices. As the enemy's arrows slashed into him, Saul could feel his blood gushing. Immanuel was long gone. All alone, he took his own sword and fell on it to end his misery.

The greatest pain is the pain of regret.

Saul had been a shy young man and had spent his life avoiding the spotlight, when God suddenly plucked him from obscurity, transformed his personality, and made him the first king of Israel at the age of thirty. This all came about as a result of the Immanuel Factor in his life.

God promised Saul that when he experienced His presence it would transform his life. And it did.

> "The Spirit of the LORD will come upon you in power, and you will prophesy with them; and you will be changed into a different person" (1 Samuel 10:6).

The shy young man became a new man. This bold leader quickly became Israel's popular king.

> When Saul heard their words, the Spirit of God came upon him in power, and he burned with anger. He took a pair of oxen, cut them into pieces, and sent the pieces by messengers throughout Israel, proclaiming, "This is what will be done to the oxen of anyone who does not follow Saul and Samuel." Then the terror of the LORD fell on the people. . . . So all the people went to Gilgal and confirmed Saul as king in the presence of the LORD. There they sacrificed fellowship offerings before the LORD, and Saul and all the Israelites held a great celebration. (1 Samuel 11:6–7, 15)

God promised to be with Saul and his young nation as long as they obeyed the Lord. But the warning was clear: Rebellion would bring rejection.

> "If you fear the LORD and serve and obey him and do not rebel against his commands, and if both you and the king who reigns over you follow the LORD your God—good! But if you do not obey the LORD, and if you rebel against his commands, his hand will be against you, as it was against your fathers" (1 Samuel 12:14–15).

### He Forgot the Secret of his Success

Unfortunately, Saul forgot where he came from and who he was without the Lord. In one instance he and his army of three thousand were under attack by a huge Philistine army. (See 1 Samuel 13:1–7.) Pressure has a way of revealing our true character, and for Saul the revelation was an ugly one. He knew he needed God's help, but he was impatient for the priest Samuel to come and secure it through burnt offerings. So as he saw his small army abandoning him and the enemy bearing down on him, he went ahead of God, disobeyed the Lord's teaching, and arrogantly acted as though he was Israel's high priest (1 Samuel 13:8–9). He tried to justify his disobedience, but God was looking for a man He could fully trust (1 Samuel 13:10–14). The manifest presence of God and the blessing accompanying it were forfeited because of his disregard for God's words.

That was tragic enough. But it got much worse for Saul.

God gave Saul and his army a great victory over the Amalekites, but Saul failed again to fully obey God. Instead of honoring God for the victory, he built a monument to himself (1 Samuel 15:1–12). When he saw Samuel coming, Saul immediately began bragging about having fully obeyed the Lord's instructions. But Samuel knew better; he confronted him with his disobedience and told him that God was grieved over how Saul, once a humble man, had forgotten God (1 Samuel 15:17). Saul rationalized his behavior, saying that he was planning a big sacrifice in God's honor, but Samuel cut him off with withering words of warning and judgment.

> But Samuel replied: "Does the LORD delight in burnt offerings and sacrifices as much as in obeying the voice of the LORD? To obey is better than sacrifice, and to heed is better than the fat of rams. For rebellion is like the sin of divination, and arrogance like the evil of idolatry. Because you have rejected the word of the LORD, he has rejected you as king" (1 Samuel 15:22–23).

The best Saul could do was to make a show of repentance. But Samuel and God would have nothing to do with his phony confession. Saul deeply regretted looking bad before his people, but he did not really care about breaking God's heart.

At this point Saul had not only surrendered the manifest

presence of God in his life but also had driven off the abiding presence of God. The rest of King Saul's reign is a sad testimony of a man trying to lead God's people without God's presence.

## Hell on Earth

Without God, life becomes gruesome and we become grotesque. This is the essence of hell—existence apart from the presence of God. The absence of God leads to the presence of Satan. For Saul, life grew increasingly ugly. It became hell on earth.

> Now the Spirit of the LORD had departed from Saul, and an evil spirit from the LORD tormented him. (1 Samuel 16:14)

I will let the scholars debate exactly what this verse means, but the message to us is obvious. Without the presence of God's Spirit, nothing will keep evil spirits from torturing us. For the rest of his life Saul fought demonic oppression and overwhelming depression.

When the next opportunity came for Saul to do something big for God, he was unable to meet the challenge. Goliath and the Philistine army intimidated Saul and his army. Saul did not have the courage to go face the giant. But David, a teenage boy living under the manifest presence of God, did. And he beat Goliath.

Instead of being grateful because God's name was glorified in the victory, Saul pouted in jealousy because the people lauded David for his courage. The next day, in fact, his jealousy became deadly in its intensity.

> Saul had a spear in his hand and he hurled it, saying to himself, "I'll pin David to the wall." But David eluded him twice. Saul was afraid of David, because the LORD was with David but had left Saul. (1 Samuel 18:10–12)

Read that last phrase again slowly: "The LORD was with David but had left Saul." Those nine words say it all. David was becoming a great success because the Lord was with him. Saul would lose it all because the Lord had left him.

The rest of Saul's life is an ugly, miserable mistake and he experienced one loss after another. He had already lost the mentoring and prayers of the high priest, Samuel. He went on to lose the popular support of his people. He ran off David, his best general, and thereby lost his valuable assistance. He surrendered the respect of his son, Jonathan, and lost the aid of his daughter, Michal, David's wife. Every battle he fought against the Philistines from then on he would lose.

Saul became a basket case. His days were clouded by fits of uncontrolled tears, unrelenting depression, unreasonable paranoia, and indefensible deeds. In murderous rages he tried to kill David on two occasions and his own son, Jonathan, once. In a despicable act of injustice and violent fury, he also irrationally ordered the murder of eighty-five innocent priests (1 Samuel 22:17–18).

Without God's presence and his general, David, Saul became paralyzed by absolute terror because he had no answer to the relentless war machine of the Philistine army. In his final hour he pitifully turned to a psychic witch for help. His final battle ended in devastating defeat. Shattered in mind, wounded in body, and crushed in spirit, Saul killed himself.

It was not the end that might have been, or the end that the prophet Samuel had promised was available to him. Yet it was the end Saul chose for himself. Only Saul could destroy his life, and he did—recklessly and completely.

The great Bible character expert Clarence Macartney summarized Saul's life with these haunting words.

> There is no braver sight than a sailing vessel under a full set of sails driving through the sea. It is the incarnation of power and grace and beauty. But there is no more dismal and melancholy sight than a shipwreck—sails gone, mast gone, rudder gone, crew gone; and the waves sounding a melancholy requiem as they break over the decks of the lost ship. Saul is a shipwreck, and when we take into consideration his

great opportunity, his many splendid traits and gifts, the greatest shipwreck in the Bible.[3]

If the image of shipwreck applies to Saul, so does the image of a castaway. Because of his own choices, he was cast away from the presence of God. After God's presence left him, Saul spent the rest of his life stranded alone on an island of torment. Paranoia, bitterness, anger, regret, and devastating depression were his only companions.

## Another Tragically Wasted Opportunity

Although the scale is less sweeping, the Bible records the sad saga of another man who began with great promise and ended in suicidal defeat. His name was Samson.

God's presence in Samson's life gave him unusual physical strength. His feats grew increasingly amazing. He ripped a lion apart with his bare hands and killed thirty enemies single-handedly. On another occasion he caught three hundred foxes, tied torches to their tails, and set them loose to burn down the Philistines' fields. Then he killed one thousand Philistines with the jawbone of a donkey.

Samson was called and supernaturally gifted by God to defeat the Philistines and liberate His people from oppression. He had been dedicated to God at birth, and his uncut hair was a symbol of his commitment. Yet selfish lust superseded godly devotion in his life. Eventually he allowed himself to be seduced by a harlot named Delilah. She tricked him into divulging the secret to his power and had someone cut his hair while he slept. When the last strand of hair was removed, the presence of God departed.

Without God, Samson was defenseless against his enemies. The Philistines took him prisoner, put out his eyes, and used him to grind grain like a dumb ox. If Saul was a shipwreck, Samson was a car crash. He started out strong and shiny, full of potential, power, and promise. But he refused to take God or God's calling on his life seriously. And his choices led to the departure of God's presence.

Yet in prison—as Samson's hair grew—humble dependence on God developed in his heart. One day the Philistines held a great sacrifice at the temple of their god, Dagon. Samson was led into the temple and chained between two pillars to entertain them. While there, he humbly asked God for renewed strength, and his prayer was answered. Because of the supernatural power of God working on his behalf, Samson was able to push two supporting pillars over, breaking down the temple and killing three thousand Philistines in the process. It was a great victory for Israel. It was one of the few things Samson did right. It was also the end of his disastrous life.

Saul and Samson made choices that put distance between themselves and the Immanuel Factor. Their choices cost them everything, and the worst part is that the awful consequences could have been avoided.

## PRINCIPLES OF THE IMMANUEL FACTOR

Just as God is irresistibly attracted to the humble, He is irrevocably repelled by the arrogant and proud. Both Samson and Saul became full of themselves and empty of God. It became all about them and what they wanted. God was neglected. When they left Him out, God left them alone. The glory departed and disaster set in.

### 1. God resists the proud.

Saul lost the presence of God when he was no longer "small in [his] own eyes" (1 Samuel 15:17) and forgot that the Lord was the secret of his success. The real secret of his success left because He was no longer valued.

The Bible is quite clear. God runs *from* the proud, but runs *to* the humble. True humility draws God like a magnet. Arrogance, conceit, pride, and self-centeredness repel God with equal force. Consider these verses:

> Though the LORD is on high, he looks upon the lowly,
> but the proud he knows from afar. (Psalm 138:6)

He mocks proud mockers but gives grace to the humble. (Proverbs 3:34)

"For whoever exalts himself will be humbled, and whoever humbles himself will be exalted" (Matthew 23:12).

"God opposes the proud but gives grace to the humble" (James 4:6; 1 Peter 5:5).

I have a friend who was one of the hottest young preachers in America at one time. He coauthored a successful book and was asked to speak all over the country—even at places like Princeton and Harvard. He often spoke to large audiences on TV. Seemingly, the sky was the limit.

God's presence ignited his teaching. When he spoke, the Bible turned from black-and-white words on a page to living color images in the minds of the audience and heart-changing conviction in their souls.

However, one day I heard him preach and I knew that something was different. Uncharacteristically, sweat poured from his brow as he obviously labored to express himself. The nature of the message and the size of the audience led us to anticipate a big response, but there was very little. I couldn't imagine what was wrong.

A couple of weeks later I found out. The news broke that he had been unfaithful to his wife. He had thought he was above the rules, but he was wrong. The anointing of God's presence on his preaching was gone.

## 2. God rejects the rebellious.

God had warned Saul that his obedience was necessary to maintain God's blessing. Saul did *most* of what God had asked, but not everything. In the eyes of God, his partial obedience was not obedience at all. It was rebellion, and no amount of sacrifice would make up for it.

Saul's sin was deeper than forgetting to do everything God asked. He had held back part of the plunder in order to honor himself. His rebellion was the manifestation of his idolatry, and his idol was himself. A heart of selfish idolatry not only rebels against God but at its core also rejects God. And God eventually rejects those who reject Him.

Without God's manifest presence, Saul had no shot at greatness. Without God's abiding presence, he became a terrible tale of tragedy.

### ARE YOU A PERSON WHO ATTRACTS GOD OR REPELS HIS PRESENCE?

God is drawn to the broken and repulsed by the arrogant. Which are you? Are you a person who attracts God's presence or repels it? The question is primarily answered by how you come down on the matter of pride or brokenness. This rugged checklist, when taken honestly, reveals areas where self-centeredness has become a God repellent. Honestly answer each question of the checklist. Where necessary, ask for forgiveness.

1. Do you think primarily about yourself when you make decisions?
2. Feel like you must have your own way?
3. Look down on others?
4. Need to prove yourself?
5. Focus on the mistakes of others?
6. Think first about your rights?
7. Desire to be served?
8. Feel driven to be recognized and appreciated?
9. Get wounded when others are recognized and you are not?
10. Think God is privileged to have your service?
11. Get defensive when criticized?
12. Work to maintain your image and reputation?
13. Find it difficult to say, "I'm sorry"?
14. Justify your mistakes and excuse your sin?
15. Only regret sin when you get caught or suffer the consequences?
16. Quickly blame others?
17. Keep people at a safe distance?
18. Use or manipulate people?
19. Expect others to take the first step of reconciliation?
20. Constantly compare and compete with others?

21. Live as though you are self-sufficient?
22. Disobey God when His will goes against what you want?

### Guarding Your Heart From Pride and Rebellion

The hot young preacher I mentioned earlier in the chapter went through a painful period of reconciliation and restoration. He honestly confronted his sins and put some protective barriers up to keep him from ever falling into sexual sin again. His marriage has been wonderfully rebuilt, and God's anointing on his preaching has returned. Instead of the extreme cockiness of his former life, he now radiates a godly humility. Several of the guidelines he adopted are as follows:

◆ *Remember who you are/were without God.*

Humility is an accurate view of oneself. Saul's downfall came because he forgot how weak and scared he had been without God in his life. When we forget that God is the best and most important thing about us, we begin to venture out onto thin ice.

◆ *Have an accountability partner or system in your life.*

Humility involves a willingness to face blind spots. Saul's life unraveled when he viewed himself as accountable only to himself. He had a potentially awesome accountability partner available in Samuel, but he did not take advantage of it. He rationalized his sin, scorned Samuel's advice, and suffered the consequences.

◆ *Learn to live a life of gratitude.*

Humility gives credit where credit is due. God took Saul from nowhere, transformed his life, and made him the first king of Israel. After crediting God with his first military victory, there is thereafter a conspicuous absence of thanksgiving and praise to God. For example, after David killed Goliath and brought Israel a great victory, Saul responded with jealousy and paranoia, not joy and praise.

The bad news is that God opposes the proud. The good news is that He pours out grace on the humble (James 4:6). As you are emptied of self, you can be full of God. And that is what the Immanuel Factor is all about.

### CHAPTER SEVEN:

# Those God Chooses and Uses
## *Humble Service*

I T'S IN YOU. It may go unnoticed or be buried for long periods of time. You may have forgotten that it is there. But the flame still flickers.

All God's children have a deep-down, inextinguishable passion to be used of God and to make a difference for eternity. The Immanuel Factor is the supernatural aid for fanning this flame.

Saul doused his passion with arrogant rebellion. Samson nearly extinguished the inner fire with water from the same bucket. But God can always find a man or woman in whom the flame burns brightly. Those are the ones He chooses to use. Those are the ones for whom He looks.

### God Looks at the Heart

After God rejected Saul, He instructed Samuel to go to the house of a man named Jesse and anoint one of his sons to become the next king of Israel. Jesse's eldest son, Eliab, looked impressive to Samuel. He was a tall, strong-willed, and striking man. When Samuel started to anoint him, God stopped him with these words:

> But the LORD said to Samuel, "Do not consider his appearance or his height, for I have rejected him. The LORD does not look at the things man looks at. Man looks at the

outward appearance, but the LORD looks at the heart" (1 Samuel 16:7).

God does not judge as man does. God does not measure a potential servant by his height or handsomeness. He measures the heart.

After Eliab was rejected, Jesse brought to Samuel his next eldest son, but Samuel shook his head no. He brought out the third oldest, but Samuel shook his head. Then the fourth oldest, then the fifth and sixth, but Samuel kept shaking his head. God was not impressed with any of them. Jesse's selection process was zero for seven. Almost comically, Samuel asked, "Are these all the sons you have?"

Fortunately, Jesse had one more son, one he had totally overlooked. This son had not even been invited into the room. He was out tending sheep. His name was David.

His own father assumed that if God was going to anoint one of his children to be king, it wouldn't be David. In the mind of his father, and initially in the mind of Samuel, David hadn't even been a consideration as somebody God would choose to use. He was undervalued, unnoticed, and overlooked by everybody . . . except God.

> So he asked Jesse, "Are these all the sons you have?"
> "There is still the youngest," Jesse answered, "but he is tending the sheep." Samuel said, "Send for him; we will not sit down until he arrives." So he sent and had him brought in. He was ruddy, with a fine appearance and handsome features. Then the LORD said, "Rise and anoint him; *he is the one*" (1 Samuel 16:11–12, emphasis added).

A short time after this King Saul dramatically descended into a pit of depression. A musician was needed to lift his spirits, and David was recommended for the position because of his outstanding credentials.

> One of the servants answered, "I have seen a son of Jesse of Bethlehem who knows how to play the harp. He is a brave man and a warrior. He speaks well and is a fine-looking man. And the LORD is with him" (1 Samuel 16:18).

The final accolade was the most important: "The Lord is with him." Even when he was a young man, the Immanuel Factor was noticeable in David's life, setting him apart. It became the distinguishing feature of his life.

A thousand years after the days of David, the apostle Paul was preaching under divine inspiration. In his sermon he gave a brief history of Israel. He described David's divine selection for the throne with these words: "After removing Saul, he made David their king. He testified concerning him: 'I have found David son of Jesse a man after my own heart; *he will do everything I want him to do*'" (Acts 13:22, emphasis added).

Just as Saul was rejected because of arrogant, self-centered rebellion, David was selected as a result of humble, God-centered obedience. God would trust David with His presence because He could trust David's heart. He knew David would fearlessly and humbly serve Him.

## PRINCIPLES OF THE IMMANUEL FACTOR

### 1. God is looking to be with people who adopt His passions as their own.

God chose David because David was a man *after God's own heart*. What does that mean?

First, it is a matter of *ownership*. David's heart belonged completely to God. He did not have any interest in other gods. He was not enamored by the idols of money, sex, or power. He had no room in his heart for ego or selfish ambition.

It also involves *commonality*. David's heart was moved by the same things that stir God's heart. God's cause was his cause.

Finally, it includes *focus*. David's heart was set on God. He always wanted more of God and continually sought to connect with Him, more often and in a deeper way.

All of these made being a person after God's own heart a matter of *obedience*. David could be counted on to serve God.

## 2. God looks for those who are actively obedient.

Paul further defined for us what it means to be a person after God's own heart when he added, "He will do everything I want him to do." The ultimate expression of being a person after God's heart is doing everything God wants you to do.

Obedience is a matter of resolve—he *will* do everything I want him to do. It is an act of the will. It is more than wanting to do right; it is willing to do right. When it came to obeying, Saul by contrast proved to be weak-willed.

Obedience involves action—he will *do* everything. The person God is attracted to is not the pacifist who sits home and never does anything wrong. It is the person out there trying to do as much right as possible.

Obedience also requires thoroughness—he will do *everything*. In God's mind, partial obedience is no obedience at all. Saul's partial obedience was viewed as complete rebellion.

Obedience seeks God's will, not self-will. God selected David because "He will do everything *I want* him to do."

## 3. God's search is unaffected by outward appearance.

Being the youngest in my family, I find great comfort in the story of David's selection. My sister is twelve years older than I am. A bright and winsome girl, my parents delighted in her. After several miscarriages, my brother's much anticipated arrival came six years later.

Then six years after my brother—an absolute surprise—I was born. Understandably, Mom and Dad were not really into parenting when I came along. They loved me, but they were tired.

Our family pictures are revealing and typical. There's a pleasant plethora of pictures of my sister as a beautiful little girl. There are also quite a few photos of my handsome older brother, the first boy, but only a few snapshots of scrawny me. Youngest children are often overlooked.

I'm just under five foot six, and I weigh 145 pounds. I was always the smallest kid in my class. In gym classes, captains sometimes have to pick their team members. If the guy doing the picking didn't know me, I was always picked last—because of my size. Anybody else know what that's like?

I totally committed my life to God as a high school student. Furthermore, a few weeks before leaving for college God called me to full-time ministry. His voice was unmistakable, but I had my doubts. Deep down, I felt that He must have made a mistake picking me for the ministry.

My first few days at a strict Christian college were a kind of culture shock for me. I had to get a short haircut. I had to lose my jeans and wear a collared shirt and tie to class. It seemed like everyone else had big black King James Version Bibles and their fathers were famous pastors. (Mine was a pale green Living Bible and my dad was an insurance salesman.)

During the first week of school there was a special chapel. The chancellor's message was titled "The Men of God for the Next Generation." At the end of his message, he introduced two amazing young freshmen. They were both only seventeen years old and had already been preaching all over America. Imagine, nationally known evangelists at such a young age! He announced that God was going to use these men for the next generation.

I remember thinking, *Compared to them, I don't stand a chance of being used by God.* One of them was tall and handsome and had a clear, captivating voice. The other was strong-looking and had an outstanding ability to speak dramatically. I was so impressed by them that I couldn't help making some comparisons. *I can't even talk in front of six people at a time*, I thought. *How can God ever use me?*

God has quite a sense of humor. A few years later He called me to plant a church. At that time the students of our school looked up (literally) to one of our graduates as the model of a church planter. He was six foot eight. He had been the star of our basketball team, an All-American. He was handsome, had a great voice, was smart, and had a fascinating testimony. I thought, *If that's what you have to be to plant a church, I am in big trouble. It is never going to happen.*

The first time I preached it was in front of an audience of about forty people. I was so nervous that I was completely flushed from the neck up; my face was bright red. Everyone thought I was angry, but I wasn't mad. I was just really scared.

Fortunately, God does not look at the outward appearance. He does not measure someone's height or handsomeness. He measures the heart.

## 4. God delights in choosing the have-nots and the are-nots.

Maybe you think you are not smart enough, strong enough, beautiful enough, talented enough, or old enough to ever be used by God. Join the club. The truth is, God delights in using people who *are not* in order to bring glory to himself. He loves to choose those who are humanly unlikely and overlooked by everyone else. Paul said it well:

> Brothers, think of what you were when you were called. Not many of you were wise by human standards; not many were influential; not many were of noble birth. But God chose the foolish things of the world to shame the wise; God chose the weak things of the world to shame the strong. He chose the lowly things of this world and the despised things—and *the things that are not*—to nullify the things that are, so that no one may boast before him. (1 Corinthians 1:26–29, emphasis added)

Look again at God's selection criteria. Human wisdom, worldly influence, and noble birth aren't what catch His eye. He is not necessarily drawn to the strong or the lofty. God calls the weak, the lowly, and especially the have-nots.

You know those six foot eight ultra-talented guys? I almost feel sorry for them, because they don't have to be God-dependent. They can probably do more in their own strength, in their own ability, and in their own power than I could ever do on my own. They may be tempted to think they don't need Immanuel. But I know I do. And so do you.

## 5. God has always worked with flawed but willing vessels.

God chooses people who understand that the key to effectiveness is not their size but His. You see, the big question is not

"How big am I?" but "How big is my God?" Those living in the manifest presence of God understand that God is big enough for anything!

God has always chosen the little, the dubious, and the blemished. Israel was a tiny chaotic collection of slaves when God chose them to be His people. Moses was a fugitive, Daniel was a slave, and so was Joseph. Amos was a farmer, and Nehemiah was a wine taster.

When God wanted a person to convey the Son of God to earth, He chose an obscure teenage girl. When Jesus needed disciples, He selected Galilean fishermen and a tax collector. When He needed resources for a miracle, He chose a little boy and his lunch. And when God wanted to replace Saul as Israel's king, He selected a young shepherd named David.

Maybe you are like me; you can think of many reasons why God wouldn't use you. You are not outwardly impressive. You don't have the right credentials. There might be a few stains on your past record. Don't worry . . . you're in good company! All of God's great heroes and heroines had gaping flaws.

Sarah's husband, Abraham, was a liar. Joseph was a convict. Moses was not only fearful but he also stuttered and had a very bad temper. Joshua was cowardly. So was Gideon. Gideon also doubted. So did Moses and Thomas. David's armor didn't fit and he was too young. Abraham was too old. Solomon was too rich, and Jesus was too poor. Peter was afraid of death, and Lazarus was dead. Yet God was with all of these people and He used them as testimonies to His grace and power.

Rahab was a harlot, Ruth a Gentile widow, and Bathsheba was an adulteress. Yet all were great-grandmothers of the Messiah.

Timothy had ulcers. Paul had bad eyes. Elijah was burned out. Jeremiah was depressed and suicidal, as was Jonah. Mary had seven demons. Hosea's wife, Gomer, was a prostitute. Paul's was a thorn in the flesh—just kidding! Abigail's husband was a jerk. Yet God blessed many people through each of them.

Abraham and Jacob both had trouble with lying. Noah had a drinking problem. Miriam was a gossip. Jonah ran from God.

Moses and Paul were murderers. Martha was a work-addicted worrier. Mary might have been a bit lazy. James and John wrestled with selfish ambition. Peter denied Jesus. The other disciples hid. John Mark was a quitter. Barnabas was a pushover. Yet God used all of them.

Originally, King Saul had attracted the presence of God because he was small in his own sight. David, overlooked and undervalued, started out knowing that he was not big enough to make it without God.

## 6. God's manifest presence is attracted and attached to humble servants.

Just as He is repelled by arrogant rebellion, God has always had a soft spot in His heart for the humbly obedient. He finds God-based humility to be an absolute magnet for His presence. Later in life David would write,

> The LORD is close to the brokenhearted and saves those who are crushed in spirit. (Psalm 34:18)

Three hundred years after this Scripture was written, God would share His heart through the prophet Isaiah. Notice that He is very clear about those He esteems most highly and with whom He wants to spend time.

> For this is what the high and lofty One says—he who lives forever, whose name is holy: "I live in a high and holy place, but also with him who is contrite and lowly in spirit, to revive the spirit of the lowly and to revive the heart of the contrite" (Isaiah 57:15).

When God looks for a place to manifest His presence, His first preference is not a glorious building. After all, He has all of the majesty of heaven in which to live. God's first choice is a human heart that is humbly obedient. He wants to be with someone who—out of true humility—takes His Word very seriously.

> This is what the LORD says: "Heaven is my throne, and the earth is my footstool. Where is the house you will build

for me? Where will my resting place be? Has not my hand made all these things, and so they came into being?" declares the LORD. "This is the one I esteem: he who is humble and contrite in spirit, and trembles at my word" (Isaiah 66:1–2).

## Keys to Humble Service

◆ *Give your heart to God.*

Humility and obedience are matters of the heart. We must acknowledge God's ownership over every aspect of our hearts.

A look into David's heart showed that all of it belonged to God. What would a look into your heart reveal?

### ACCESS TO EVERY ROOM IN OUR HEART

In 1954, Robert Munger wrote a booklet designed to help college students better understand what it meant to give Jesus their whole heart. *My Heart, Christ's Home* is a meditation on the reality that as Christians, Christ comes into our lives and wants to be "at home" in our hearts. In it, Munger writes a very convicting narrative of a man who learns what it really means to give Jesus everything by allowing Him into *every* room of his heart.

He had to choose to let Jesus control his thoughts, dominate his appetites, and use his gifts. He had to learn not to allow busyness to crowd Jesus out of his life. And he even had to be willing to open the door to the secret areas of his heart. Eventually, he asked Jesus to take over the responsibility of his whole house, his whole heart, and make his life what it ought to be.

Although He was willing to do this, Jesus faced an obstacle. He was only a guest, and He lacked the authority to effect change. When He made this known to the man, the man wasted no time. Dropping to his knees, he transferred the title of his home to Jesus and submitted himself to be His servant.

"Lord, You have been a guest and I have been the host. From now on I am going to be the servant. You are going to be the owner and Master."

The man ran as fast as he could to his strongbox and took the title deed of the house describing its assets and liabilities, location and situation. He eagerly signed the house over to Jesus for time and eternity, saying,

"Here it is, all that I am and have, forever. Now You run the house. I'll just remain with You as a servant and friend."

He found this was the best way to live a Christian life. "Things have been different since Jesus has settled down in my heart."[1]

◆ *Serve God actively*.

Humble obedience is not a passive attitude. It is a matter of vigorous action. Obedience is more than not doing bad things. It is aggressively doing good things. It is doing all God wants you to do.

### DETERMINED TO ACT ON WHAT HE BELIEVED

William Wilberforce was a twenty-five-year-old English politician when he was converted to evangelical Christianity. He knew that his new commitment might cost him friends and influence, but he was determined to act on what he now believed.

His friend John Newton (writer of the song "Amazing Grace") persuaded him that his political life could be used for the service of God. His faith required him to act. So Wilberforce set out to "renew society."

He became the conscience of the British parliament. He said that God gave him two great objectives, the renewal of society and the end of slavery. He spent the rest of his life taking action to defend the children of the poor and to maintain the cause of those who had no helper.

He obeyed the prompting of God and wrote a popular book, calling on the upper classes to regain true Christian values in their lives. He organized the Society for the Suppression of Vice. Wilberforce also worked in the Association for the Better Observance of Sunday. The result was the prototype of a Sunday school, its goal to provide all children with regular education in reading, personal hygiene, and religion.

He was a major supporter of programs for popular education. Overseas missions, parliamentary reform, prison reform, medical aid for the poor, education for the deaf, restrictions on the use of child labor, aid for the deaf, religious liberty, action against gambling, and the establishment of the Royal Society for the Prevention of Cruelty to Animals were all part of his extraordinary legacy. One estimate suggests that sixty-nine causes were significantly advanced by Wilberforce's efforts. One biographer, John Pollock, was surely right when he said that Wilberforce was a "man who changed his times."[2]

But the primary area of his activism was in his lifelong, lonely, and unpopular battle to have slavery abolished in England. Understanding the brutal nature of the battle, the great Christian leader John Wesley once wrote to Wilberforce, "Unless God has raised you up for this very thing [abolition], you will be worn out by the opposition of men and devils. But if God be for you, who can be against you?"[3]

Eventually his efforts paid off. Three days before he died, in 1833, Wilberforce heard that the House of Commons had passed a law emancipating all the slaves in Britain's colonies. A year later nearly one million slaves were set free.

At his funeral he was honored with this statement by William Hague,

> Wilberforce, more than any other man in his generation, exemplified in his life how to translate a religious calling into political action.[4]

Although committed to political action and parliament's work, Wilberforce knew that political change would not bring Britain *lasting* success. He wrote:

> [The best hope for Britain is not] in her fleet and armies, not so much in the wisdom of her rulers, but in the spirit of her people and in the persuasion that she still contains many who, in a degenerate age, love and obey the Gospel of Christ.[5]

## ONE CONCERNED WOMAN CAN MAKE A BIG DIFFERENCE

In 1978, Beverly LaHaye watched a television interview of radical feminist Betty Friedan, founder of the National Organization for Women. Realizing that Friedan claimed to speak for the women of America, Beverly LaHaye was stirred to action. She didn't believe that the radical feminists' anti-God, anti-family rhetoric represented her beliefs, nor those of the vast majority of American women. So in spite of her retiring nature, she began to educate and alert Christian women on such issues as the Equal Rights Amendment. The response was overwhelming. This became the springboard for a national organization called Concerned Women for America.

The organization's mission is to protect and promote biblical values among all citizens, first through prayer, then education, and finally by influencing our society. Members hope thereby to reverse the decline in moral values in our nation. LaHaye and an army of women have worked tirelessly to carry this out as they have stood on the front lines in support of biblical values before our government. Today, twenty-five years later, Concerned Women for America is a vibrant organization with well over five hundred thousand members spread across all fifty states, and which is coordinated by a dynamic staff from its national office in Washington, D.C.

### FINDING YOUR PLACE OF HUMBLE SERVICE

God has a place for all of us to serve. There is a need, a ministry, a cause that must become our calling to fulfill.

Do you have a heart to obey God's call to serve?

Where do you need to take action?

What has God told you to do?

In what area should you stand up and speak up?

### CHAPTER EIGHT:

# "Ain't It About Time Sumbody Dun Sumthin'?"
## *Fearless Initiative*

F OR MORE THAN A DECADE central Ohio radio listeners tuned into 610 WTVN daily to hear the gravelly voice of fictional character Billy Ray Vulgar rant and rave about some societal ill or pet peeve. His down-home observations on local situations and national issues were wickedly insightful and often extremely humorous. Every day he would complete his venting by signing off with his trademark, "Ain't it about time sumbody dun sumthin'?"

One day I was speaking to my church on some aspect of active discipleship and found myself getting carried away. The next thing I knew, out of my mouth popped the question, "Ain't it about time sumbody dun sumthin'?" It's bad in terms of grammar, but it is a valid question. Life in the manifest presence of God is unavailable to the passive. It is only experienced by those who *do* something. It is only enjoyed by the fearless initiators.

This was another difference between David and Saul. When opportunity came, Saul slunk away from it, but David embraced it. And God showed up.

The Philistine army in general, and a giant named Goliath in particular, were intimidating Israel. As the two armies faced each other, with the Valley of Elah between them, a challenge was thrown out. The challenge centered on a battle-by-champion showdown, with the winner's side taking all. The stakes were high because "taking all" included the defeated soldiers becoming subjects to their enemy. Goliath, the nine foot six Philistine giant, would take on Israel's champion (1 Samuel 17:1–10). And Israel's champion should have been Saul. He stood a head taller than any other Israelite (1 Samuel 10:23) and was an accomplished warrior. The only trouble was, Saul no longer had the presence of God. He couldn't count on a victory, so he was hiding in his tent, terrified by Goliath's challenge.

But David had the Lord with him. He wasn't afraid.

## PRINCIPLES OF THE IMMANUEL FACTOR

### 1. God's manifest presence is on the battlefield.

Unlike all the others, David did not run from the battle. He did not stand on the sidelines and watch. He ran to the fight.

> David left his things with the keeper of supplies, [and] ran to the battle lines. (1 Samuel 17:22)

While all the Israeli soldiers waited for someone else to step out, David stepped up. He said to Saul, "'Let no one lose heart on account of this Philistine; your servant will go and fight him'" (1 Samuel 17:32).

You see, David had learned a secret Saul had forgotten. David knew that the manifest presence of God was not with those cowering in safety out of the enemy's reach. God's presence was (and is) on the battlefield. He goes with us when we are taking risks for His name and His cause. God is with those who fight His battles. So in spite of the fearful doubters around him, David exercised faith and volunteered to take on Goliath.

> Saul replied, "You are not able to go out against this Philistine and fight him; you are only a boy, and he has been a fighting man from his youth."
>
> But David said to Saul, "Your servant has been keeping

his father's sheep. When a lion or a bear came and carried off a sheep from the flock, I went after it, struck it and rescued the sheep from its mouth. When it turned on me, I seized it by its hair, struck it and killed it. Your servant has killed both the lion and the bear; this uncircumcised Philistine will be like one of them, because he has defied the armies of the living God" (1 Samuel 17:33–36).

Notice the source of David's confidence. "This uncircumcised Philistine will be like one of them, because he has defied the armies of the living God." David knew that God goes with those who go out to face God's foes. A lot of people truly desire the blessings and benefits of the manifest presence of God in their lives, but they don't want to inconvenience themselves. They are sadly addicted to their comfort zone. They fear pain, hardness, or difficulty. They want to sit on the sidelines and soak in God.

But God is not there!

God is on the *front* lines, not the sidelines.

As Saul and the Israeli army huddled a safe distance away, fearful of facing Goliath, they did so without God. He was not there. He was waiting out in the field of battle for somebody to join Him. When we step out fearlessly for God, He is there to fight with us.

## 2. God's manifest presence gives confidence to the God-centered.

Taking God and a slingshot with him, David ran to face Goliath. The giant warrior saw him, laughed, and licked his chops. But the Lord was with David; so David answered his taunts boldly.

David said to the Philistine, "You come against me with sword and spear and javelin, but I come against you in the name of the LORD Almighty, the God of the armies of Israel, whom you have defied. This day the LORD will hand you over to me, and I'll strike you down and cut off your head. Today I will give the carcasses of the Philistine army to the birds of the air and the beasts of the earth, and the whole world will know that there is a God in Israel. All those gathered here will know that it is not by sword or spear that the LORD saves; for the battle is the Lord's, and he will give all of you into our hands" (1 Samuel 17:45–47).

David's response is a wonderful portrait of a man living in the fullness of the Immanuel Factor. Every sentence is totally God centered and faith filled. He came against Goliath "in the name of the LORD Almighty, the God of the armies of Israel." He was certain the Lord would use him to defeat the giant. The purpose of this battle was that "the whole world will know that there is a God in Israel." He confidently stated that the Lord would prove to be mightier than the sword, spear, or javelin because "the battle is the Lord's"—and He always wins His battles.

David showed incredible courage and confidence because he knew that this was God's cause, and he had the advantage of the Immanuel Factor.

As a pastor I have seen God's presence provide His people with astonishing bravery to face extremely stressful and difficult situations. My dad wrestled with terminal bone cancer for a year. Yet he faced each day with a bright smile and an optimistic outlook because "the Lord is with me." My friend Verna also had cancer and was in a great deal of discomfort. But she always spoke with such confidence and courage because, as she said, "the Lord is with me, giving the peace that passes understanding."

### 3. God's manifest presence is the determining factor in spiritual battles.

Without God's presence, it would have been an extreme mismatch. Goliath, the gigantic veteran warrior, would, in the natural, have crushed David, the teenager. It looked hopeless, and it was . . . for Goliath. The Lord was with David, and one plus God is a majority. His presence is the "odds buster," the guarantee of victory.

Fighting for the cause of God with the presence of God is the only way to win victories for Him.

> As the Philistine moved closer to attack him, David ran quickly toward the battle line to meet him. Reaching into his bag and taking out a stone, he slung it and struck the Philistine on the forehead. The stone sank into his forehead, and he fell facedown on the ground.
>
> So David triumphed over the Philistine with a sling and a stone; without a sword in his hand he struck down the Philistine and killed him.
>
> David ran and stood over him. He took hold of the Philistine's sword and drew it from the scabbard. After he killed him, he cut off his head with the sword. When the Philistines saw that their hero was dead, they turned and ran. (1 Samuel 17:48–51)

Because the Lord was with him, David killed the giant and Israel won the battle. David became the hero Saul should have been and could have been—had he not lost the presence of God.

### 4. God's manifest presence is activated through fearless initiative.

When David got out of his comfort zone and moved forward for the cause of God, he found that God was *already there*. Sure, David was a good shot, but no man—let alone a raw teenager facing a giant warrior in front of two watching armies—would have been able to get off a decent shot, let alone a perfectly placed one, without the presence of God.

#### ONE PLUS GOD IS ALWAYS THE MAJORITY

A few hundred years after David's reign in Israel, the rough-hewn prophet Elijah was the only one willing to confront the wicked idolatry of King Ahab. Risking death, Elijah confronted Ahab and challenged him to gather the people for a power duel of deities. The gathered nation watched the contest to see which god—Jehovah or Baal—had the power to ignite a sacrifice on fire in response to prayer.

When the day of decision came, Elijah stood alone on Mount

Carmel, facing four hundred and fifty prophets of Baal and four hundred prophets of the goddess Asherah. The odds were eight hundred and fifty to one! It looked like a mismatch, and as it turned out, it was.

One plus God is always a majority. That day God was not on the sidelines with the crowd, watching to see what would happen. He was out there with Elijah every step of the way. In a dramatic display of power God showed up, big time. He ignited a soaking wet sacrifice into a blaze that sent the enemy running (1 Kings 18).

### Living a Life of Fearless Initiative

1. *Go where God is.*

If you want to be with God, you need to go where God is. The story of the Bible is the story of an active God, who is a risk taker. He is not a passive observer of life. He is a highly creative being, who did, does, and *will do* great things. If we want to experience such a God, we must go where He is.

GOD IS NOT IN THE BOAT

Jesus sent His disciples off without Him and stayed back to pray. Out in the midst of the Sea of Galilee, the disciples found themselves trapped in a storm. Jesus came to their rescue, walking on the water. Never having seen such a thing before, they were pretty shook up. Jesus reassured them and told them they had no reason to be afraid.

If seeing Jesus walking on water was not bizarre enough, what happened to Peter next was even more bizarre.

> "Lord, if it's you," Peter replied, "tell me to come to you on the water."
> "Come," he said.
> Then Peter got down out of the boat and walked on the water to Jesus. But when he saw the wind, he was afraid and, beginning to sink, cried out, "Lord, save me!"
> Immediately Jesus reached out his hand and caught him. "You of little faith," he said, "why did you doubt?"

And when they climbed into the boat, the wind died down. Then those who were in the boat worshiped him, saying, "Truly you are the Son of God" (Matthew 14:28–33).

When we read this story, we tend to focus on Peter taking his eyes off Jesus and sinking. We are reminded that faith comes from looking at Jesus, and not at the waves crashing around us. This is a good application of the Scripture. However, for those of us interested in discovering keys to the manifest presence of God, something else is much more important: Peter, just an ordinary guy, actually *walked on water*—but not until he had the guts to get out of the boat and head for Jesus. Sure, he got a little wet, but what a thrill! He was walking on the water with Jesus! Yes, it was a risk, but he got to experience the entire thing—including the hand of Jesus rescuing him—while the other guys in the boat let fear rob them of this awesome opportunity.

Jesus is not often in the safety of the boat. He is usually out on the water in the storm. If we want to experience nearness with Jesus, we must go where He is.

I find that I rarely experience God in the comfortable times and convenient places of life. I have felt His presence most unmistakably when I have been willing to get out of the boat of comfort. I have really encountered His presence when the storm is raging and the waves are crashing.

In her book *The Hiding Place*, Corrie ten Boom tells of her awful ordeal in a Nazi prison camp during the Second World War. Trying to survive the unspeakable horrors of Ravensbruck Concentration Camp, Corrie and her sister, Betsie, found that as they risked greater deprivation and beatings in order to share Jesus with the other prisoners and even some of the guards, the presence of Jesus was an unmistakable reality. He miraculously spared their Bible from being confiscated and kept their vitamins from running out. And He shone contagiously from their filthy faces.

After she was released from prison, Corrie found the presence of Jesus to be just as real as she launched out in a ministry of healing and housing people who were scarred by the war. God went with her as she ventured out to travel the globe, sharing her stories about Jesus being the Victor in every situation she faced.

### Jesus Is With the Needy

If you want to find God, go *where God is*. He can be found among those who are most needy.

Mother Teresa learned the secret of experiencing the manifest presence of God as she followed Jesus and allowed His compassionate heart to direct her steps. In 1979, the world honored her with the Nobel Peace Prize for her sacrificial work in India.

Thirty years earlier, the tiny nun left all semblance of a comfortable life and fearlessly started a home in the worst place imaginable for the people she called the "Dying Destitutes." By faith, she began a ministry that eventually touched hundreds of broken souls each day in India and inspired thousands of others around the world.

When she received the Nobel Prize, she said her ministry was "to the hungry, the naked, the homeless, the crippled, the blind, the lepers, people who feel unwanted, unloved, uncared for throughout society, and all those people that have become a burden to the society and are shunned by everyone."[1]

It was among the poorest of the poor that she experienced the vast treasures of the rich manifest presence of God. She said she felt closest to God as she ministered to the destitute. Once she described the resulting joy by saying, "When I wash the lepers' feet, I feel I am nursing the Lord Himself. Is that not a beautiful experience?"[2]

### Our God Is an "Out There" God

God's heart is out there—with the destitute, the broken, and the needy. He is with the hurting and the lost. God's heart is with the children and the aged. He is an "out there" God. He is out of the boat, off the sidelines, and *in the battle*. Those who have experienced the most of God are those who are most "out there" with Him.

Maybe your circumstances restrict you from packing up and moving to India, facing a bunch of false prophets, or challenging a giant in battle. You probably have not been sent to prison for your faith. But you can still go out where God is. You can travel on your knees.

In the last few years I have had the privilege of speaking at an annual conference to some of the greatest heroes on earth, missionaries to the least reached peoples on the planet—Muslims, Hindus, and Buddhists. Also at these gatherings are retired missionaries. Some of these folks are no longer able to physically minister in Iran, Iraq, Turkey, or China, but that does not hold them back. They go out there every day—on their knees in prayer.

You can too.

2. *Take the initiative.*

Sometimes we spend so much of our time and energy focused on avoiding and eliminating the evil from our lives that we miss the opportunity to do good. I agree with Erwin McManus when he writes,

> I am convinced that the great tragedy is not the sins that we commit, but the life that we fail to live. You cannot follow God in neutral. God created you to do something.[3]

"You cannot follow God in neutral." Too often we merely sit, waiting for something to happen, and wonder why it never does. If you sense God is in something, *go for it*. Put your energies in gear and go for it. Act. Move. Reach. "God created you to do something." So . . . do it.

At Thanksgiving this year, I asked my sons to evaluate what had happened in the past few months and tell me when they felt closest to God during that time. We had enjoyed some powerful services in our church, but that was not what came to their minds. Instead, all three of them said they felt closest to God when they were leading our evangelistic Bible study for high school students. Doing something for God put them in the place of depending on God, and God is near to those who trust Him.

## 3. *Embrace the now.*

David could have stood with the rest of the non-soldiering soldiers and recounted how he had killed a bear and a lion in the past, but that would not have done anyone any good. Instead, he took confidence from his past and launched out into the present.

Past success is often the cause of failing to experience God in the present. We try to hold on to what we already have and in the process miss what could be. But God is not in the past. He exists in the present moment. He lives in the here and the now. Theologians will tell you that God lives outside the realm of space and time. He does not exist in the past or the future but in a never-ending present. The only thing He knows is *now.* If we want to experience God, we must embrace the opportunities of the now.

In spite of doing what some have viewed as crazy, my friends Jamal and Ed have launched a church at Ohio State University among secular university students. In this unlikely place of radical godless thought, wild drinking, and casual sex, they have seen God passionately at work to win this needy generation of young adults. Jamal and Ed love to be a part of that.

And Ken believes that God wants him to launch a church in the culture and arts section of our city. There among the tattoo parlors, the vulgar gift shops, and the trendy restaurants staffed with gay waiters, he believes God is just waiting to bust out in the now. And He is.

## 4. *Be willing to take a risk.*

I live in Columbus, Ohio. City leaders like to call us "The Discovery City." Thinking about discovery causes one truth to become strikingly clear. In order to discover new lands, people must leave their home shores. There is no discovery without risk. The Immanuel Factor is there to be discovered, but it won't happen without risk on your part.

Henry Blackaby writes, "You cannot continue life as usual or stay where you are, and go with God at the same time."[4]

That is proved true throughout Scripture.

- ◆ Noah could not continue life as usual and build an ark at the same time.
- ◆ Abram could not stay in his hometown of Haran and fulfill God's promise to make of him a great nation in the land of Canaan.
- ◆ Moses took a risk when he left a cushy job in his father-in-law's business to obey God's command to go and confront Pharaoh, ordering him to let God's people go.
- ◆ Joshua took a risk when he stepped into the Jordan River, believing that it would open up so that he and his people could cross it. It was also at great risk that he ordered them to march around the walls of Jericho seven times, blowing trumpets, as commanded by God.
- ◆ Rahab turned her back on a lucrative prostitution business in order to follow God.
- ◆ Ruth risked the familiar to strike out with her mother-in-law for a foreign land.
- ◆ Gideon took a risk to face an army of thousands with only three hundred men.
- ◆ David had to leave his sheep to become Israel's king.
- ◆ Elijah took a risk when he faced eight hundred and fifty wicked prophets on Mount Carmel and challenged them to a prayer duel.
- ◆ Esther put her life on the line to save her people.
- ◆ Amos had to leave the sycamore trees in order to preach in Israel.
- ◆ Jonah had to leave his home and overcome a major prejudice in order to preach in Nineveh.
- ◆ Peter, Andrew, James, and John had to leave their fishing business in order to follow Jesus.
- ◆ Matthew had to leave his tax collector's booth to follow Jesus.
- ◆ Saul (later Paul) had to completely change direction, facing persecution and suffering for the rest of his life, in order to bring the gospel to the Gentiles.

5. *Act on your godly passions.*

David's prime passion was God. When Goliath began to mock the cause of God, David had no choice. He had to fight him. His passions demanded nothing less. So he acted on his godly passions and joined God on the field of battle—and brought down the giant Goliath. David did what he felt compelled to do.

### He Had to Take a Stand

Five hundred years ago, Martin Luther, a young German monk, was reading the Bible and found salvation through faith in Jesus Christ. From that moment on his passion was the gospel. So it should be no surprise that when he saw the truth of the gospel being lost through the misuse and abuse of a works religion, he took action. Just as a seminary student might nail his dissertation to his professor's door, Martin Luther nailed his Ninety-five Theses to the door of his church. He knew that such a deed could bring a death sentence, but he did it anyway.

God is with those who take fearless initiative for His cause. Luther's act helped bring about a titanic shift in Western world history, culture, and religion. The spark of the hammer hitting the nail touched off the Protestant Reformation.

When brought to trial for his deed, Luther refused to give in, saying,

> "Unless therefore, I am convinced by the testimony of Scripture . . . I cannot and will not retract. . . . Here I stand, I can do no other. So help me, God. Amen."[5]

And God did help him. Protestant churches around the world trace their roots to that one fearless action. Luther did what he did because he had to.

Everyone who has ever made a difference through the Immanuel Factor was a person of passionate clarity and fearless initiative. As God stirred up desires in them, they acted on their godly passions. They refused to sit back and watch. They got off the bench. They ran onto the field. They got out of the boat.

They did something. And God was with them all the way.

What is it that God has placed within you to do? What is the passion that He has inscribed on your heart? Find it. Act on it. And enjoy the presence of God as you do.

CHAPTER NINE:

# God Seekers
## *Passionate Pursuit*

T HE WEEK BEFORE I MET CATHY, I came up with what I considered to be a brainstorm. I was a student at a Christian college with only ten weeks left in the semester. Knowing that I might never have as good a chance to get to know so many attractive Christian girls again, I made a list of the ten girls I wanted to date. I planned to ask out one girl each week of the ten weeks. It would be a delightful dating odyssey.

But then I met Cathy. That brief encounter ruined my plan. She jumped to the number one spot on my list and was my date the next nine weekends in a row.

I wanted to know all I could about her. I wanted to be with her as much as possible. But that was more difficult than it might seem. I lived on campus, which was located on a mountain outside of town. She lived in town with her sister. Neither of us had a car. My dorm had eighty young men and one telephone. I wondered how I would ever get to know her better.

But, amazingly, it seemed like every time I came out of class, she just happened to be nearby, heading to her class. It was weird. I had never seen her before, and now she was there all the time. *What good luck*, I thought!

It wasn't until after we were married that I heard her laughing with one of her girlfriends. She was telling her how she had worked for the dean of the School of Religion and had used her position to get a copy of my schedule so she could "just happen" to be outside of all my classes when they let out.

I was stunned to realize that while I thought I was pursuing her, in actuality, *she was pursuing me.* She skillfully positioned herself so I would think that I was pursuing her. When I first found this out, I was a little angry about her duping me all along. But after thinking about it, I was highly grateful that she had gone to all that trouble to get to know me.

A few days later I was praying and telling God that I was seeking after Him with all my heart. I was inwardly almost proud of my pursuit. Then it hit me. Just as Cathy allowed me to think I was the pursuer when I was actually being pursued by her, God does the same thing. We think we are discovering God, when, surprisingly, He is there all along, skillfully positioning himself just within reach, waiting to be found by us.

God is there to be found. Our divine Lover is there to be loved. God does not hide from us. He wants to be found.

You can find Him. David did.

## The Secret of His Success

After crushing Goliath, David became an instant success and the darling of the masses. He continued walking with God, and God continued to bless him. The presence of God brought him prosperity, protection, and popularity. He won battles and gained fans . . . and it tore Saul apart (1 Samuel 18:1–9). As we read in the last chapter, David's success and Saul's failure could be attributed to one thing: the Immanuel Factor.

> Saul was afraid of David, because the LORD was with David but had left Saul. So he sent David away from him and gave him command over a thousand men, and David led the troops in their campaigns. In everything he did he had great success, because *the LORD was with him.* When Saul saw how successful he was, he was afraid of him. But all Israel and Judah loved David, because he led them in their campaigns. (1 Samuel 18:12–16, emphasis added)

> When Saul realized that *the LORD was with David* and that his daughter Michal loved David, Saul became still

more afraid of him, and he remained his enemy the rest of his days. The Philistine commanders continued to go out to battle, and as often as they did, David met with more success than the rest of Saul's officers, and his name became well known. (1 Samuel 18:28–30, emphasis added)

God's presence made David a success. David's success drove Saul even crazier than he was already. As the above verse states, Saul chose to become David's enemy for the rest of his days. From that moment on Saul was intent on killing David. For nearly a decade he and his army hunted David through the Judean wilderness, hoping to catch him and kill him. David had to leave behind his position, his wife, his home, his friends, and his reputation as he ran for his life. But he did not go alone. The Lord went with him.

The next few years of David's life were filled with nail-biting episodes of narrow escape. Yet he was not afraid. He found the manifest presence of God to be the antidote to anxiety and the prescription for overcoming fear. What is interesting is that Saul had an entire army with him, yet he was afraid of David. David, on the other hand, was alone yet completely fearless. This was because the Lord had left Saul but was with David.

How did David cultivate such a close companionship with God? What led to the steady release of God's presence in his life, with its accompanying power on David's behalf?

Happily for us, we do not have to guess, because David was a prolific and gifted writer. His journal records his growing relationship with God. These writings were set to music and became the core of the Hebrew songbook. We know them as the Psalms. A study of his writings reveals the secrets to David's unusual ability to cultivate and maintain the manifest presence of the Lord in his life.

## PRINCIPLES OF THE IMMANUEL FACTOR

### 1. The manifest presence of God envelops those who live a God-centered life.

As you know, David spent his early years tending his father's sheep. This meant long periods alone in the wild. It was here that David developed the familiar friendship and delightful devotion to God that is the heart of experiencing the Immanuel Factor. It was while out tending the sheep that David began to passionately pursue God and seek His presence.

Looking back on this time in his life, David wrote what have become some of the most familiar and beloved words ever penned. Read them slowly through the lens of the Immanuel Factor.

> The LORD is my shepherd, I shall lack nothing. He makes me lie down in green pastures, he leads me beside quiet waters, he restores my soul.
>
> He guides me in paths of righteousness for his name's sake. Even though I walk through the valley of the shadow of death, I will fear no evil, for *you are with me*; your rod and your staff, they comfort me.
>
> You prepare a table before me in the presence of my enemies. You anoint my head with oil; my cup overflows. Surely goodness and love will follow me all the days of my life, and I will dwell in the house of the LORD forever. (Psalm 23, emphasis added)

My Hebrew teacher taught us that the most important thought in a Hebrew sentence is stated first. Likewise, the most important idea in a psalm is stated in the first sentence. The first words of the first sentence of the twenty-third psalm give us the key to the psalm. And they also show us the heart of the author and how his focus invited the Immanuel Factor. The key words are "The LORD."

For David, it all started with the Lord. If he had the Lord, he had everything. And without the Lord, he had nothing. Because of the Lord, he would not be in want, even when he was on the run. With the Lord, he would receive the guidance he needed to elude Saul and stay alive.

Since God was with him, David did not need to fear evil, or even death. Even though he was surrounded by enemies, God's presence would comfort and provide for him, befriend him, and bless him abundantly.

Even in the worse situation imaginable, David experienced a very close relationship with God. This is because the priority in his life was the Lord; the passion of his life was being with Him, and the primary pursuit in his life was their relationship.

## 2. The manifest presence of God stabilizes those who train their minds on Him.

> I have set the LORD always before me. Because *he is at my right hand*, I will not be shaken. (Psalm 16:8, emphasis added)

"I will not be shaken" is a marvelously bold statement, speaking of the powerful protection provided by God's presence. When he said this, David was speaking from experience. Saul and his army had chased him for years through the Judean wilderness. Even though David found himself trapped many times, in each case God protected him and provided him with a narrow escape.

David was fearless because he knew that God was a greater ally than Saul was a foe. He saw God as being at his right hand. In the chaos of battle it is vital to have a companion fighting alongside you, watching and defending your unprotected places. This is what is implied by the phrase "at my right hand."

How did David get God to be at his right hand? It was simple. He said, "I have set the LORD always before me." God was central in his thoughts.

### PRACTICING THE PRESENCE

Nicholas took a winding path to the presence of God. He became a soldier, then a footman, a cabinet officer, and finally, a monk. Large and clumsy, he was put to work in the stables before ending up in the only job in the monastery he couldn't mess up—helping in the kitchen. Here, with God as his only companion, he became the keeper of a powerful secret, the secret of Immanuel.

Nicholas, or Brother Lawrence, as he came to be known, loved God with all his heart. He set a goal for himself to *practice* the presence of God all day long. After years of such practicing, his life was so positively transformed and his inner spiritual vitality so deep that a high-ranking church leader sought him out as his spiritual director. Their four conversations, along with sixteen letters that contained his insights into living in the manifest presence of God, were eventually combined into a book. This devotional classic is called *The Practice of the Presence of God*.

Like David, Nicholas had a God-centered mind. He said, "I make it my only business to persevere in His holy presence, wherein I keep myself by simple attention, and an absorbing passionate regard to God."[1] He used his devotions as a means to an end: living in the presence of God.

Brother Lawrence discovered that the way to sense God's presence all day was to have lots of conversations with Him. In fact, he thought it was shameful to cut off a conversation with God. His goal was to form the habit of talking to God all the time. The key was continually loving God and recognizing Him as intimately present with us, and therefore addressing Him with every thought.[2]

Like David before him, Nicholas learned to set God always before him. He trained his mind to continually turn to God. He gave very helpful advice when he wrote, "Hold yourself in prayer before God like a poor, dumb, paralytic beggar at the rich man's gate. Let it be your business to keep your mind on the Presence of the Lord."[3]

3. **The manifest presence of God is near to those who turn to Him in their brokenness.**

David's loyalty to Saul was returned by Saul's murderous paranoia. The king that David deeply desired to serve tried to kill him and chased him from his beloved nation. Heartbroken, he fled for his life.

The best hiding place is usually the last place anyone would ever think to look for you. Where could David hide from his own king and his army? With their enemy the Philistines, of course. Unfortunately, when David went to Achish, the king of Gath, some of Achish's servants recognized him. "Isn't this

David, the king of the land? Isn't he the one they sing about in their dances?" (1 Samuel 21:11).

Trapped and desperate, David prayed, and came up with a strange plan: He pretended to be insane. And because of the Lord's presence with him, it worked. The Philistine king said he had enough madmen bothering him and did not need another. So David left Gath and escaped to the cave of Adullam (1 Samuel 21:12–22:1). While in this cave he recorded what he had learned through his near-death adventure. We find his insights in Psalm 34.

> The righteous cry out, and the LORD hears them; he delivers them from all their troubles. *The* LORD *is close* to the brokenhearted and saves those who are crushed in spirit. (Psalm 34:17–18, emphasis added)

David found out that the Lord draws near to deliver the crushed who cry out to Him. The Immanuel Factor goes to work for the heartbroken. The hotline to God's presence is the desperate prayer of the downtrodden. This is how David expresses it:

> I sought the LORD, and he answered me; he delivered me from all my fears. Those who look to him are radiant; their faces are never covered with shame. This poor man called, and the LORD heard him; he saved him out of all his troubles. The angel of the LORD encamps around those who fear him, and he delivers them. (Psalm 34:4–7)

When David recounted the story of his deliverance, he could not help but make a reference to the Immanuel Factor and the resulting glow of God: "Those who look to him are radiant."

Psalm 142 is described as "A maskil of David. When he was in the cave. A prayer." Doesn't that make perfect sense? The only sensible thing to do when you are holed up hiding in a cave is to pray!

> I cry aloud to the LORD; I lift up my voice to the LORD for mercy. I pour out my complaint before him; before him I tell my trouble.

When my spirit grows faint within me, it is you who know my way. In the path where I walk men have hidden a snare for me. Look to my right and see; no one is concerned for me. I have no refuge [in men]; no one cares for my life.

I cry to you, O LORD; I say, "You are my refuge, my portion in the land of the living." Listen to my cry, for I am in desperate need; rescue me from those who pursue me, for they are too strong for me. (Psalm 142:1–6)

The first statement clues us in that this is not your basic bow-your-head-and-quietly-think-nice-thoughts-about-God prayer. This is a loud, urgent, emotional outburst. As we saw earlier in the life of Moses, David had a deep enough relationship with God to be raw and emotional with Him. So when grave trouble came to David, desperate turning to God came out of him.

God is our Father and our friend. Out of the depth of relationship, the natural tendency of God's people should be to turn urgently to God when trouble comes. David was a man who lived in the manifest presence of God. He didn't hesitate when adversity hit; he turned to God.

## ANYWHERE WILL DO

David turned to God while in a cave. But we can turn to Him anywhere we happen to be when we need help. In one of his books, author Max Lucado tells of a woman who turned to God late one night when she was lost and alone on a New York City subway.

"She had missed her [stop] on the subway. By the time she realized her mistake, she didn't know what to do. She prayed for safety and some sign of God's presence. This was no hour or place for an attractive young woman to be passing through a rough neighborhood alone. At that moment, the doors opened, and a homeless, disheveled man came on board and plopped down next to her. *God? Are you near?* she prayed.

"The answer came in a song. The man pulled out a harmonica and played, 'Be Thou My Vision'—her mother's favorite hymn.

"The song was enough to convince her. Christ was there, in the midst of it all."[4]

## 4. The Immanuel Factor is released to those who thirst after Him.

Psalm 63 bears a short, simple title: "A psalm of David. When he was in the desert of Judah." This reveals nothing of the turmoil, trauma, and trials that David faced as he fled for his life and hid out in the desert, but within the psalm we see clearly both his anxiety and his passion for God. The very first verse reveals the secret of David's ability to live in the manifest presence of God.

> O God, you are my God, earnestly I seek you; my soul thirsts for you, my body longs for you, in a dry and weary land where there is no water. (Psalm 63:1)

The first words out of David's mouth and the foremost thought on his mind is God. David was unashamedly God centered and God thirsty. He did not cry out for justice, vengeance, or deliverance. He was not asking for food, drink, or shelter. He yearned for God, thirsted for God, and pined for God alone.

This was David's secret. This is the passion of those throughout all time who seek and find God—a burning, relentless, undeniable thirst for Him.

### TEN DAYS OF SERIOUS THIRST

In high school I was on the wrestling team. High school and collegiate wrestling is an intensely demanding and disciplined sport. The beauty of the sport is that competitors wrestle people who are their own size. The agony of the sport is dropping weight in order to be more competitive.

During my senior year in high school I injured my knee and missed a month in the middle of the wrestling season. Because of the resulting inactivity of this recovery time, I gained quite a bit of weight. A doctor's visit brought surprising news—both good and bad. The good news was that my knee had healed more quickly than expected. I would be able to wrestle a match in ten days! The bad news was that I had only *ten days* to lose the seventeen pounds I had thought I would have three weeks to lose.

Those ten days were the most difficult of my life. I ran three miles before school and wore triple layers of sweat suits in practice. I cut down to tiny meals and determined to drink only twenty-four ounces of fluid a day. The weight came off quickly the first few days, but after that it slowed down considerably. My fluid levels got so low I could hardly break a sweat.

It wasn't food I craved. It was liquid. My parched mouth was a desert, and my tongue felt like it was made of cotton. At night I tossed and turned, dreaming of waterfalls and rivers. I imagined thrusting my hands into a tub of ice and pulling out a bottle of Orange Crush in each hand. I would awake counting the minutes until I could drink again. Thirst made me crazy, weak, irritable, light-headed, and slow-moving.

When I finally hit the weight I was aiming for, nothing could hold me back. I bolted off the scale and grabbed a large can of Hi-C. Never before had I ever drunk so excitedly or with so much gratitude. Then I ate a couple of oranges and gulped a few glasses of water. But I still felt like I couldn't get enough fluid.

God seekers thirst after God like I thirsted after fluid. They think about, dream about, and long for Him alone.

David's long, lonely days on the run in the wilderness gave him an intense longing for God. Just as a man who is lost for days in the desert passionately seeks an oasis, David passionately sought God. He thirsted, yearned, craved, desired, and chased after God. And he found Him.

> I have seen you in the sanctuary and beheld your power and your glory. Because your love is better than life, my lips will glorify you.
>
> I will praise you as long as I live, and in your name I will lift up my hands. My soul will be satisfied as with the richest of foods; with singing lips my mouth will praise you.
>
> On my bed I remember you; I think of you through the watches of the night.
>
> Because you are my help, I sing in the shadow of your

wings. I stay close to you; and your right hand upholds me.
(Psalm 63:2–8)

God is a person. Like any person, He wants to go where He
is wanted. He likes to be where He is liked and loves to be where
He is loved. God allows himself to be caught by those who chase
Him. And He manifests His presence in the lives of those who
seek Him like that.

## How to Passionately Pursue God

David's example reveals four simple keys for effectively pursuing God. Adopt them into your own life.

- Center your life in God.
  Let the Lord be the beginning and the end, the core and
  the foundation. Don't let God be merely an afterthought.
  Make Him your first thought.
- Train your mind on God.
  I had a friend in college who set his alarm to beep qui-
  etly every hour. Why? To remind him to think about God.
  Train your mind to turn toward God in prayer or praise all
  through the day.
- Take your problems to God.
  Problems can cause us to run either *from* God or *to* Him.
  Decide to use your problems as prompts to run to God in
  prayer.
- Thirst after God.
  Instead of getting full of other things, stay lean and hun-
  gry for God. Cut out other distractions and pursue the pure
  presence of God. One God seeker, Buddy Owens, shared
  how this works in his life.

  I can honestly say today that I am continually aware of
  his presence. And I am also aware of my growing hunger for
  more of him. I live in the paradox of having found God, or
  rather having been found by him, yet having to always
  search for him. . . . I sense God's presence not because he
  decided to show up, but because I decided to make myself
  available to him.[5]

### CHAPTER TEN

# The Real Raiders of the Lost Ark
## *Reverently Undignified*

I HAVE TO ADMIT THAT I AM a sucker for the Indiana Jones movies, especially the first two. When they are on TV, I just have to watch them. I think the thing that is so compelling is that Indiana Jones is so determined that he will pursue the prize no matter how difficult or how costly the effort may be.

The first movie, *Raiders of the Lost Ark*, is my favorite because it is about the effort to secure the lost ark of the tabernacle. Indy finds himself caught in the middle of a diabolic attempt of Nazi Germans to secure the ark because of the incredible power it would bring to its possessor. Hitler reasons that with the ark on his side, his armies would be invincible.

One of the reasons I like that movie so much is because the Bible goes back three thousand years and tells the true story of another adventurer and treasure hunter that could be called Israeli David.

Yet unlike Indy Jones, who sought the ark because of its historic value, or the Nazis, who wanted to harness its power, David wanted the ark because it contained and localized the manifest presence of God.

David had experienced the power, prosperity, provision, and protection of the presence of God unlike any man of his generation and few other men of any generation. God had taken him from shepherd boy to court musician to warrior hero to general to king's son-in-law to fugitive to king. He knew that if his fledgling nation had a chance to survive it would be because of the manifest presence of God. *He had to have it.*

Soon after becoming king, David sought to return the ark of the covenant to Israel. It had been lost to the Philistines during the carnal days of Eli (1 Samuel 4). What the Philistines did not know when they captured it was that Immanuel, the presence of God, does not bless the wicked. When they put their new "good luck charm" and trophy next to their god, Dagon, God knocked the statue of Dagon on its face before the ark of the covenant.

Thinking it was an accident, the Philistines put the statue back up next to the ark. But the next day they found it in the same place—on the ground before the ark of the Lord, this time with its head and hands broken off! (1 Samuel 5:1–5) In an amazing display of power, God's Spirit brought one devastation after another to the Philistines, until they were anxious to return the ark to its rightful owners (1 Samuel 5:6–7:1).

The ark was a wooden box, four feet long, two feet wide, and two feet deep. At that time the small, gold-plated wooden chest was the place where the manifest presence of God resided. There His glory shone as a laser beam from heaven above the small cherubim affixed to the top of the ark. When it was placed in the Holy of Holies in the tabernacle, God's presence rested above it as a cloud by day and a fire by night. It was the most localized manifestation of the presence of God on planet earth.

David desperately desired this holy piece of furniture be returned to his people. Its return would usher in the return of God's presence and resulting blessing upon the land. For this reason he was determined to bring it home.

> He and all his men set out from Baalah of Judah to bring up from there the ark of God, which is called by the Name, the name of the LORD Almighty, who is enthroned between the cherubim that are on the ark. (2 Samuel 6:2)

The ark would symbolize a return of the presence of God to

His nation Israel. Their efforts to secure the ark serve as a guide to the type of worship that secures the manifest presence of God.

## PRINCIPLES OF THE IMMANUEL FACTOR

"Yet you are enthroned as the Holy One; you are the praise of Israel" (Psalm 22:3). In reference to this verse, Jack Taylor says:

> Praise is where God lives. His habitation is with hot, holy, hungry-hearted worshipers. His presence is manifested greatly when He is worshiped rightly.[1]

David's endeavor to return the ark to Jerusalem is a wonderful guide to the role of public worship in releasing the manifest presence of God. The type of worship that secures the Immanuel Factor must be worship that reflects energy, exacting reverence and abandonment.

### 1. The possibility of God's manifest presence unleashes energetic praise.

Since its return from the Philistines (it had been too hot for them to handle), the ark had been residing temporarily eleven miles southwest of Jerusalem, under the care of Abinadab.

Filled with anticipation and excitement at the prospect of retrieving it, David spared no trouble or expense. Soldiers, priests, and much of the nation joined him in a huge, zealous, energetic, vigorous gala before the Lord. Every musical instrument they could find was included in the festivities as the ark was carted home.

> They set the ark of God on a new cart and brought it from the house of Abinadab, which was on the hill. Uzzah and Ahio, sons of Abinadab, were guiding the new cart with the ark of God on it, and Ahio was walking in front of it. David and the whole house of Israel were celebrating with all their might before the LORD, with songs and with harps, lyres, tambourines, sistrums and cymbals. (2 Samuel 6:3–5)

Some people say that because they have subdued personalities, they should not be expected to get "all worked up" in worship to God. But I don't buy that line anymore. Watch how those same subdued people act when their favorite sports team wins the big game in overtime or when they win some jackpot. See how subdued they are then as they jump up and down, yelling and slapping high-fives. Big events bring out big emotions, and such was the case in 2 Samuel 6.

Some of us grew up in churches that struggle with the notion of high-octane praise and worship. The church where I attended began each worship service with "The Lord is in His holy temple, let all the earth be silent before Him," sung in solemn tones by a choir of somber-faced people. As a teen, I took that as my cue to go to sleep.

Certainly there are times when we should approach God in an awestruck hush and draw near to Him with reverent stillness. There are also times when we are to bow low before Him with tears and groans, mourning over our sins . . . but not *all* the time.

Worshiping the living God with lifeless worship is nonsensical. Worshiping Almighty God without energy or vigor simply doesn't fit.

The ark of God had been in enemy hands for several generations, since the tragic last days of Eli the priest (1 Samuel 4:17–22). When the Philistines carted off the ark, the glory of the Lord departed from Israel. Now the entire nation was rightly celebrating its return. Their emotions overcame them as their joy overflowed into energetic celebration.

## 2. The holy power of God's manifest presence requires exacting reverence.

"At the Hanover plutonium separation plant in eastern Washington, plutonium and U–235 are kept in a special high-security vault, in brass cans wrapped three times in plastic. To move the radioactive material, specially trained handlers don white protective overalls and special breather masks. They never touch the materials except through a sealed 'glove box.' These rigid rules grew out of hard experience. For years no one knew the dangers of radioactivity. . . . Gradually scientists realized: If you are going to use the atom, you must adopt procedures to fit its power."[2]

If special precautions are necessary for working with atomic energy, extraordinary precautions are vital when people dwell with God. He is infinitely more powerful than radioactivity, an atomic power plant, or a nuclear bomb. He is the ultra-holy, almighty God. He is "a consuming fire" (Hebrews 12:29). If we are not careful, we could get burned.

The ark of God was the most supremely precious and surpassingly holy item on the planet. God dwelt there. Hence, it contained phenomenal power. It could bring amazing blessing or extreme destruction. Seventy men died when they carelessly peeked inside (1 Samuel 6:19). Therefore, so that no one would be hurt, God gave careful instructions as to who could touch it and how it was to be handled and transported.

> "This is the work of the Kohathites in the Tent of Meeting: the care of the most holy things. When the camp is to move, Aaron and his sons are to go in and take down the shielding curtain and cover the ark of the Testimony with it. Then they are to cover this with hides of sea cows, spread a cloth of solid blue over that and put the poles in place. Over the table of the Presence they are to spread a blue cloth and put on it the plates, ladles and bowls, and the jars for drink offerings; the bread that is continually there is to remain on it. Over these they are to spread a scarlet cloth, cover that with hides of sea cows and put its poles in place. . . . After Aaron and his sons have finished covering the holy furnishings and all the holy articles, and when the camp is ready to move, the Kohathites are to come to do the carrying. But *they must not touch the holy things or they will die*" (Numbers 4:4–8, 15, emphasis added).

Sincerity and energy are not enough in dealing with atomic power—or the presence of God. It is possible to be sincere, but be sincerely wrong. It is possible to misplace your energy. David and the nation of Israel discovered this the hard way.

Foolishly, David had rushed out ahead of God, without

consulting Him, to bring the ark back to Jerusalem. He failed to follow the instructions that had already been laid down by God. As a result, people were hurt.

> When they came to the threshing floor of Nacon, Uzzah reached out and took hold of the ark of God, because the oxen stumbled. The LORD's anger burned against Uzzah because of his irreverent act; therefore God struck him down and he died there beside the ark of God. (2 Samuel 6:6–7)

All the air was sucked out of the party. After two miles of intense celebration, all the joy suddenly vanished, extinguished by sorrow and fear. Oh, the details . . . the right people, covering the ark carefully, and transporting it the right way. *What is the big deal with the details?* we might ask. *The Lord can't be that concerned about the details, right?* Wrong!

Israel was just getting started as a nation. Worship was to be such an integral part of their lives that they would have to get it right from the beginning. They needed to start with such healthy respect and high esteem for God that they would even take care with the details.

God does care about the fine print. The little things may make a big difference. For Uzzah, a few details made the difference between life and death.

There is great danger in being too careless about God and the things of God. As His people, we must learn to take God more seriously and take ourselves less seriously. When God says something is important, we need to make it important to us as well.

Jesus said that the road to God and the abundant life of the Immanuel Factor is a narrow, detailed, difficult road.

> "Don't look for shortcuts to God. The market is flooded with surefire, easygoing formulas for a successful life that can be practiced in your spare time. Don't fall for that stuff, even though crowds of people do. The way to life—to God!—is vigorous and requires total attention" (Matthew 7:13–14 THE MESSAGE).

David desperately wanted the presence of God to bless his

people (2 Samuel 6:11–12). So he researched the details carefully. To his credit, David did not give up on his quest after the first attempt to retrieve the ark failed. And to his further credit, the next time he read the instructions first and carried them out exactly. For three months he scoured the country, looking for priests and planning the proper way to transport the ark. When he had the right people committed to doing it the right way, he launched out again (1 Chronicles 15:13–15).

3. **The unlimited glory of God's manifest presence evokes uninhibited exuberance.**

David was a colorful person and engaging personality because he was an all-or-nothing type of guy. If God was worthy of praise, then he would praise God with everything he had. If God wanted details, then David would give Him details—and then some. He also would give God serious sacrifice and unrestrained enthusiasm because he knew God was worth it.

So for a second time, the giant gathering of priests, the massive array of the army, and a huge crowd of people all launched out together to bring the ark back to Jerusalem. But after only six steps it all came to a halt. A bull and a calf were sacrificed to God. Why? Because He is worth it.

> So David went down and brought up the ark of God from the house of Obed-Edom to the City of David with rejoicing. When those who were carrying the ark of the LORD had taken six steps, he sacrificed a bull and a fattened calf. (2 Samuel 6:12–13)

After the sacrifice, the parade cut loose. Choirs were singing, instruments were playing, banners waved in the wind, the people cheered, and King David danced with all his might.

> David, wearing a linen ephod, danced before the LORD with all his might, while he and the entire house of Israel brought up the ark of the LORD with shouts and the sound of trumpets. (2 Samuel 6:14–15)

### THE JOY OF WITNESSING THE UNSEEN

A few months ago I was visiting West Point Military Academy for a football game. I had low expectations going to the game. West Point is a highly academic, buttoned-down, East Coast military academy. Cadets wear uniforms to class and salute their instructors. Their football team, the Black Knights, had lost nineteen games in a row and was playing one of the top teams in their league. The forecast called for rain. The experts predicted a blowout for the visiting team.

But walking through the gate just moments after the opening kickoff, I was transported to euphoria. Just as the sun burst triumphantly through the clouds, the crowd erupted, the cannon boomed, and the earth shook. Miraculously, the Black Knights had just scored a touchdown! Forty thousand people were standing, jumping, clapping, laughing, and cheering.

Then, before the crowd could calm itself, the impossible occurred—right before our very eyes—they scored *another* touchdown. There had not been such a celebration in that stadium for years.

Packed on one side of the stadium were four thousand cadets dressed in army fatigues and black shirts, all delirious with happiness and drunk with joy. They customarily stand on the bleachers during the entire home game to cheer for the Black Knights. But for this game, their euphoria was so high they seemed to be hovering above the bleachers.

Cadets always cut loose on Saturday afternoon home games because they have been tied down with studies and military restrictions all week long. But the enthusiasm they expressed at the game that day was several levels above the norm. They were witnessing what was before unseen. The Black Knights had not won a home game in four years. In other words, none of these cadets had seen a home game victory. Now they were up 14–0 before the first quarter was over! It truly was too good to be true!

I can imagine the emotional release that erupted from David and his people as they brought the ark home would rival the emotion shown by West Point at their incredible game. They too were witnessing the before unseen. The ark had been out of their country for three generations. None of them had ever seen it. None had felt the power of the presence of God that emanated from it. They had only heard the stories.

Priests who had only dreamed of ministering near the Holy of Holies would now have the opportunity. God seekers who had longed to pray where they might feel the presence of God would be able to do so.

And David . . . David already knew the power of the manifest presence of God on his life. It surrounded him and protected him. And now he would finally share it with his people!

As a man after God's own heart, David was quite relieved to have the details in order and God well pleased with him again. To him, nothing was sweeter than the smile of God's pleasure, because it brought the radiance of His presence.

Beyond that, this was a once-in-a-lifetime opportunity. Once the ark was returned to its proper place—in the most secure part of the tabernacle—only the High Priest would be able to approach it. And even he would do so only once a year. But on this day, *all* of Israel had a chance to see the ark and to stand in the presence of Almighty God.

It was too much—such joy meant that David truly could not contain himself. He was right with God, and God was right there with him. The day he had imagined for so long had finally arrived. The ark of the presence of God was safely back in Jerusalem to lend to all the people God's abundant blessings. Is it any wonder that the king got a little carried away?

But sadly, some people just didn't get it.

**4. The mystery of God's manifest presence totally escapes those who are halfhearted.**

As the ark of the LORD was entering the City of David, Michal daughter of Saul watched from a window. And when she saw King David leaping and dancing before the LORD, she despised him in her heart. They brought the ark of the LORD and set it in its place inside the tent that David had pitched for it, and David sacrificed burnt offerings and fellowship offerings before the LORD. After he had finished sacrificing the burnt offerings and fellowship offerings, he blessed the people in the name of the LORD Almighty. Then he gave a loaf of bread, a cake of dates and a cake of raisins to each person in the whole crowd of Israelites, both men and women. And all the people went to their homes. When David returned home to bless his household, Michal daughter of Saul came out to meet him and said, "How the king of Israel has distinguished himself today, disrobing in the sight of the slave girls of his servants as any vulgar fellow would!" (2 Samuel 6:16–20).

## REASONS SOME PEOPLE JUST DON'T GET IT

◆ They have never personally experienced "it."

God loves you with an abandoned, uninhibited, undeniable, relentless, passionate, extravagant love. At those times when you get carried away with God's love, you cannot help but get carried away in worship. But until you have deeply experienced the love, grace, mercy, power, and touch of God, you will never understand exuberant worship.

This wasn't the only time in Scripture that someone disdained uninhibited worship. One night Jesus went to dinner in the courtyard of a Pharisee's house. When a woman who had lived a sinful life in that town learned that Jesus was eating there, she came too, bringing with her an alabaster jar of perfume. As she stood behind where He was reclining she was overcome with emotion. Weeping profusely, she wet his feet with her tears. Then she wiped them with her hair, kissed them, and poured the perfume on them (Luke 7:37–38).

Her extravagant, undignified worship elicited indignation and contempt from Jesus' host. The self-righteous Pharisee just didn't get it. He had never tasted the sweet waters of mercy and the wonderful wine of forgiveness. Because he did not think he needed Jesus, he couldn't make any sense of her uninhibited expression of love and gratitude.

◆ They have never laid down the god of self.

David was not *self*-conscious because at the moment of celebration he was totally God conscious. What was going on wasn't about him—it was all about God.

But it was the exact opposite with Michal. David's actions embarrassed her and affected her reputation.

Her eyes were so focused on herself that she totally missed God. She was so caught up in the horizontal that she missed the vertical. Her mind was so stuck on the temporal that she completely overlooked the once-in-a-lifetime opportunity to step for a moment into the joys of the eternal.

She had never felt the need to give her whole heart to the Lord. Other gods also occupied her life (1 Samuel 18:20; 19:13). The Lord was just one of many gods in her life, and all of them were secondary to the god of self.

◆ They have never given God control.

Worshiping the Lord was all right with Michal—as long as it was restrained, discreet, dignified, and under control. More than anything else, she feared losing control. So her motto was "Don't get carried away."

By contrast, David, her own husband and the new king, got totally transported in worship. He completely lost control. His wild dance and lively leaps were too much for her to fathom or stomach. So she criticized him through her sarcasm.

**5. The manifest presence of God is released when we live for an audience of one.**

When his own wife greeted him with a vicious stream of sarcasm, David was unmoved by her attack. She was not his audience. God was.

> David said to Michal, "*It was before the* LORD, who chose me rather than your father or anyone from his house when he appointed me ruler over the Lord's people Israel—I will celebrate *before the* LORD. *I will become even more undignified than this, and I will be humiliated in my own eyes.*" (2 Samuel 6:21–22, emphasis added).

David's undignified celebration was because he saw himself as worshiping solely before God and no one else. There is amazing freedom in learning to live for an audience of one and choosing to please God in spite of the negative reaction of men.

There is a glorious release when we become people who are God centered and not self-centered, God conscious and not self-conscious. Not only does it release us from ourselves and the control of others, but it also releases God to us, which is even better. God shows up when He knows that He is the only one in the audience.

In this story, who was right—the dignified Michal or the undignified David? If there were any doubts, they are dispelled by the next verse. God judges Michal severely for her attitude.

> And Michal daughter of Saul had no children to the day
> of her death. (2 Samuel 6:23)

It goes without saying that barrenness is not a judgment from God in most cases. There are all sorts of reasons, many of them physiological, for not being able to conceive. But in this particular case with Michal, Scripture does seem to indicate that her subsequent barrenness was the result of her unfair and critical attitude toward David's unabashed enthusiasm for God. She picked the wrong person to try to condemn and humiliate—God was quick to come to His servant's defense and to erase all questions about which heart pleased Him more.

### Securing the Presence of God in Worship

♦ Let your love for God break out of your mind, into your heart, and run through your body. Don't be afraid to give God enthusiastic praise.

♦ Use everything at your disposal to worship God.

♦ Be sure that your life and worship are in line with God's Word, will, and ways. Read the fine print. Dot the *I*'s and cross the *T*'s.

♦ Be willing to allow the immense dignity, majesty, and glory of God to "undignify" your life. Then really worship.

◆ Become so God conscious that you lose your self-consciousness.

Let me encourage you to approach your next opportunity to experience corporate praise and worship with a fresh level of anticipation. Start praying about it now. Concentrate as each word of each song is sung. Be aware that God is there, willing to pour out His love, grace, and power to all who really want Him.

### CHAPTER ELEVEN:

# Here's Me!
## *Wholehearted Commitment*

B OTH WERE YOUNG CHICAGO SALESMEN. Marshall dedicated his life to the business of making money. He opened a store in Chicago bearing his name, and in time it made him Chicago's most powerful man. One of America's richest businessmen in the nineteenth century, he amassed a fortune of over $120 million in his lifetime. His name, Marshall Fields, is still known as one of America's most famous retail store empires.

Unlike Marshall, Dwight was a salesman who was becoming more and more dissatisfied with the business world. His real passion was serving God. One day he heard a quote that changed his life and the lives of many others: "The world has yet to see what God will do with and for and through and in and by the man who is fully consecrated to Him."

"He said 'a man,'" thought Moody. "He did not say a great man, or a learned man, or a smart man, but simply 'a man.' I am a man, and it lies with the man himself whether he will or will not make that entire and full consecration. I will try my utmost to be that man."[1]

He was not well educated, and he never amassed a business empire. But Dwight took over a Sunday school class of twelve kids and grew it to fifteen hundred *before his twenty-third birthday*. And in time he had a church that was influential throughout the world.

Over the course of his life, Dwight was used of God to

preach to some of the largest evangelistic gatherings ever known in England and the United States. Over one million souls were converted! He didn't leave behind a store bearing his name, but a college carrying the name Moody has trained thousands of young men and women to change their world with the gospel of Jesus Christ.

God used Dwight L. Moody in a manner disproportionate to his education or background. He only had two outstanding qualities—a burning passion to be used of God and a willingness to be fully committed to Him. But they were more than enough in God's hands.

God loves to show himself strong on behalf of any man or woman who is fully committed to Him. He wants to use you beyond your wildest imagination. King Asa found this out. Let him show us how.

## A Mixed Message

Asa's father, Abijah, had a short but eventful reign as Judah's king. In an interesting aspect of Scripture, First Kings describes King Abijah as a disloyal, halfhearted follower of the Lord who kept idols in the land and refused to give God all of his heart. As a result, his reign was filled with war (1 Kings 15:3–6).

On the other hand, Second Chronicles shows him at his best, chastising Jeroboam for his idolatry and boasting of his refusal to turn his back on God. When outnumbered in battle, Abijah wholeheartedly relied on God and the presence of the Lord brought him a stunning victory (2 Chronicles 13:4–18).

### A WISE CHOICE

Asa saw both aspects of his father's commitment to the Lord and was attracted to his father's positive side—trusting and following God. To Asa's credit, he began his reign wholly committed to God. He did what his father had failed to do. He tore down altars to foreign gods, cut down their images, and commanded his people to worship and obey the Lord. When an army of one million Ethiopians and three hundred chariots came against him and his five hundred and eighty thousand men, Asa took his problem to the Lord.

Then Asa called to the LORD his God and said, "LORD, there is no one like you to help the powerless against the mighty. Help us, O LORD our God, for we rely on you, and in your name we have come against this vast army. O LORD, you are our God; do not let man prevail against you" (2 Chronicles 14:11).

The presence of the Lord is attracted to wholehearted commitment and total reliance. In response to Asa's prayer God came and gave him a great victory.

The LORD struck down the Cushites before Asa and Judah. The Cushites fled, and Asa and his army pursued them as far as Gerar. Such a great number of Cushites fell that they could not recover; they were crushed before the LORD and his forces. The men of Judah carried off a large amount of plunder. (2 Chronicles 14:12–13)

God was pleased with what He had seen of Asa's heart. He wanted to encourage him to continue. So God sent a message to Asa that contained a powerful promise—a promise that applies to us as well.

"Listen to me, Asa and all Judah and Benjamin. The LORD is with you when you are with him. If you seek him, he will be found by you, but if you forsake him, he will forsake you. . . . But as for you, be strong and do not give up, for your work will be rewarded" (2 Chronicles 15:2, 7).

## A CONTINUED COMMITMENT

Asa took the Lord's encouragement to heart and continued leading his nation toward God. He removed idols from wherever he had jurisdiction. He renovated the aging altar of the Lord in the temple. Then he called his nation together for a great time of sacrifice to the Lord. This event climaxed when they all made a public pledge of wholehearted commitment.

They entered into a covenant to seek the LORD, the God of their fathers, with all their heart and soul. . . . They took an oath to the LORD with loud acclamation, with shouting and with trumpets and horns. All Judah rejoiced about the oath because they had sworn it wholeheartedly. They sought God eagerly, and he was found by them. So the LORD gave them rest on every side. (2 Chronicles 15:12, 14–15)

Later, in an extreme display of his total commitment to the Lord, Asa removed his own grandmother from the position of Queen Mother because she had made a large idol. Then, like David, he brought consecrated gifts to God in the temple. The Bible summarizes his life with these words: "Asa's heart was fully committed to the LORD all his life" (2 Chronicles 15:17).

## A Big Mistake

As long as Asa was totally committed to the Lord he was blessed with victory, peace, and prosperity. But at the end of his life Asa let outside pressures influence him, causing him to go back on his commitment to the Lord. Here's what happened.

Asa's kingdom of Judah was on the eastern edge of the Mediterranean Sea. Just north of them was Israel, which was then under the leadership of an idol worshiper, King Basasha. Above Israel was the nation of Aram.

Israel's king was causing problems for Asa. Instead of relying on the Lord's help, as he had in the past, Asa came up with a scheme of his own. He hired the king of Aram to attack Israel so Israel's attention would be drawn away from Asa's kingdom. His plot worked, but God was not impressed. He sent the following message to Asa through one of His prophets.

"Because you relied on the king of Aram and not on the LORD your God, the army of the king of Aram has escaped from your hand. Were not the Cushites and Libyans a mighty army with great numbers of chariots and horsemen? Yet when you relied on the LORD, he delivered them into your hand" (2 Chronicles 16:7–8).

God told Asa that his scheme had cost him the opportunity to do away with his potential enemy once and for all. Now the hand of the Lord's protection and peace would be removed.

"For the eyes of the LORD range throughout the earth to strengthen those whose hearts are fully committed to him. You have done a foolish thing, and from now on you will be at war" (2 Chronicles 16:9).

Unfortunately, Asa did not respond well to this message. Instead of acknowledging his sin and repenting, he got angry and vented his rage in ugly and unprofitable ways. "Asa was angry with the seer because of this; he was so enraged that he put him in prison. At the same time Asa brutally oppressed some of the people" (2 Chronicles 16:10).

### A POWERFUL PROMISE

In the flow of the story it is easy to skip over the heart of the message God gave Asa. It's found at the beginning of verse 9. Let's look at it again, more closely.

"For the eyes of the LORD range throughout the earth to strengthen those whose hearts are fully committed to him" (2 Chronicles 16:9).

God is looking to reward those who are totally committed to Him. The blessing begins with the prize of His presence. When God shows up, all of His strength comes with Him.

God is on a search; He is looking for you. God is not looking for people of knowledge; He already knows everything. He is not looking for people of wealth; it all belongs to Him anyway. He is not impressed with talent or strength; He is the Almighty. God is searching for people who are *wholeheartedly committed to Him*. Those are the ones He loves to hang out with and use for His glory. Those are the ones for whom He powerfully manifests His presence.

## PRINCIPLES OF THE IMMANUEL FACTOR

### 1. The Immanuel Factor provides peace and rest (2 Chronicles 14:6; 15:15).

Asa was able to strengthen and build his nation, as was Solomon before him, because the presence of the Lord granted him rest from his enemies. Other nations refused to attack.

We face spiritual enemies in the form of lying demons and oppressive spirits. But when God's around, Satan leaves town. God's presence can provide us with wonderful seasons of peace and rest *from* enemy attack. And sometimes He gives us peace and rest *in the midst of* attack.

## 2. The Immanuel Factor gives victory against overwhelming odds (2 Chronicles 14:9–15).

Asa's army was outnumbered two to one by a vastly superior army. Yet God's presence brought them a dominating victory over a superior force.

Many of us wrestle with bad habits and besetting sins. Or we have been given human legacies of defeat or shame. We need to remember that the presence of the Lord is the essential ally in giving us victory and making us more than conquerors.

## 3. The Immanuel Factor makes the type of leader people want to follow.

> Then he assembled all Judah and Benjamin and the people from Ephraim, Manasseh and Simeon who had settled among them, for large numbers had come over to him from Israel when they saw that the LORD his God was with him. (2 Chronicles 15:9)

God-fearing people flocked to Asa when the Lord's presence became evident in his life. It marked him as a man of God and a leader who would lead effectively.

Many who aspire to leadership, and even those already in leadership positions, often overlook the obvious. We get caught up in the business world's teachings about success and forget that the manifest presence of the Lord is the essential foundation for effective leadership. It is God's presence in our lives that gives us godly influence in the lives of others.

## 4. The Immanuel Factor is conditionally experienced (2 Chronicles 15:2).

We are only as close to the manifest presence of the Lord as we really want to be. If we draw near to God, He will draw near to us. If we want to be with Him, He will be with us. God is always willing and available. The decision is ours.

Both times that God sent word directly to Asa it had to do with the conditional nature of the manifest presence of God. God would be with him, *if* he would commit to be with God.

## 5. The Immanuel Factor is released through full commitment (2 Chronicles 16:9).

God promises His strength to those who have given their whole heart to Him. If God only has a little bit of our heart, we only get to experience a little bit of His presence. If God has all of our heart, we get to experience all of His presence. The more God has of us, the more we get to experience Him.

HERE'S ME!

In one sense, she had nothing necessary to make a difference for God. Barely five feet tall, Gladys Aylward had been a shop girl, a nanny, and a parlor maid. The daughter of a mailman, she only had a basic education and no formal religious or ministry training. But on the other hand, she had *everything* a difference maker needs. She had the manifest presence of God.

One day she read a story about China and the need for missionaries there. At the age of twenty-eight Gladys sensed a deep burden to make a difference in China. She applied to the China Inland Mission, only to be rejected because of her lack of missionary training.

Dejected, she sat in her maid's quarters and emptied her purse on top of her Bible. Two pennies fell out. Then she gave herself wholeheartedly to God, saying, "O God, here's my Bible. Here's my money. Here's me!"[2]

God can't resist a heart wholly dedicated to Him. Soon He opened the door for her to go to China under the auspices of a tiny independent mission. She saved as much money as possible and took the cheapest route to China—on the rugged Trans-Siberian Railroad. After a close brush with death, she finally arrived in northern China.

The missionary she was to stay with died soon after Gladys

arrived, but not before an inn was opened for Chinese mule drivers. On her own, Gladys taught herself the language and began to minister to the rough mule drivers the only way she knew how—by telling them Bible stories. Amazingly, they listened.

She came to be called Jen Ai', "the one who loves people." God's presence spread her impact, reaching even into the Chinese government when she was able to lead the local mandarin to Christ. She also touched the lives of many children while she was there. When the Japanese invaded Shanghai, Gladys was enabled, by the presence of God, to lead one hundred refugee children a great distance over dangerous mountains to safety.

When illness forced her to return to her home in England, Gladys was invited to dine with royalty, including the Queen. She spoke to the largest churches in the country. The Oscar-winning actress Ingrid Bergman portrayed Gladys's life story in the popular movie *The Inn of the Sixth Happiness*. The film was nominated for an Academy Award and won a Golden Globe Award. Gladys Aylward's story continues to touch people's lives with the message that God will greatly use and bless those who are fully committed to Him.

## GIVING ALL OF MYSELF

My parents were faithful Christians. Since birth I had been in church every Sunday. And like many evangelical children, I accepted Jesus Christ as my personal Savior while in elementary school. Unfortunately, after the first few months of excitement, I did not grow much. Other than on retreats, at church camp, or on Sunday mornings, most of the time I did not even think of God.

As a high school student a battle for control of my life waged. A few of my friends were sold out to Jesus and on fire for God. I wasn't. At best, God was just another part of my life. He certainly did not hold a central place in my heart. There were sports, friends, art, school, music, books, my ten-speed bicycle, family, and God—pretty much in that order. And I was miserable.

God designed each of us with a gaping God-shaped void in the center of our heart. While we will have other things in our lives, the center was made especially for God. Nothing else quite fits there. Life doesn't quite click until God is given the central place. I knew I should commit all of my life to Jesus, but I rationalized that I couldn't live the Christian life . . . so why should I try?

At the beginning of my junior year the Holy Spirit was making my God-shaped void painfully obvious. My on-fire Christian friends seemed to glow with a God-given sense of satisfaction that I sorely lacked. My plan, which included trying one thing after another as the center of my life, was not working. It left me restless and frustrated.

One Sunday as church began, I slid into my seat in the very back row at the top of the balcony, as far away from the action as possible. Tired from delivering a hundred newspapers earlier in the morning, I was hoping to go to sleep when the singing was over. Before I did, I happened to glance down at a Sunday school paper I had been handed on my way out of class that day. A sentence in a box at the bottom of the page caught my attention: *"Commitment is giving all that you know of yourself to all that you know of God."*

It was as if a laser beam illumined those words to me. I read them again. *"Commitment is giving all that you know of yourself to all that you know of God."*

*That's simple enough,* I thought. *It doesn't say that I must become a missionary or give all my money to the poor or witness to everybody at school. It doesn't say that I have to become perfect or immediately have all the answers. It doesn't say that I will never have fun again.* I read the words again.

Then a voice whispered in my head, *"That's what you need to do. You can do it. I will be there with you."*

That evening I sat on the floor of a big old house along with several dozen other kids. The previous couple of Sunday nights a few of my sold-out friends had talked me into attending youth group. It had been much better than I expected. Some kids played guitars, and we sang some praise choruses. The youth pastor gave a Bible study.

The most challenging part of going there was listening to the on-fire kids give testimonies of how God was working in their lives. They seemed so happy and full as they spoke of God being with them as they witnessed to their friends. It made me feel empty, because they obviously had something going with God that I did not have.

All night one thought kept going through my head, the one I had read that morning: *"Commitment is giving all that you know of yourself to all that you know of God."*

At the end of the evening, when we bowed our heads to pray, a silent prayer thundered from my heart.

> *God, I want you to be with me like you are with those other kids. I am sorry that I have been resisting you for so long. Forgive me. Right now, as best as I know how, I give all of me to all of you. If you will have me, I am yours. I don't want you to just be a piece of my life; I want you to be the center of my life. Let's take this one day at a time. Amen.*

Peace. Warmth. Love. Joy. Those elusive blessings had finally filled my heart.

What I felt most was peace, poured like liquid gold down into my heart by the gallon. For the first time since I had gotten saved I felt really full inside. I was full of peace and love and joy, but mostly I was full of God.

I was blessed speechless.

The next few days at school, I knew God was with me—and He made such a difference. I was so full of joy that some people asked if I was high on drugs. Suddenly I had the power to resist temptation. I was no longer lonely. And I was not afraid or ashamed to talk to people about Jesus.

Amazingly, many students came to Christ through me. Within a year up to one hundred public high school students joined me and a friend for a daily lunchtime Bible study. Most of the girls on the Homecoming court got saved, as did most of the young men on the wrestling team. Truly God manifests His presence mightily wherever He finds hearts totally committed to Him.

## Wholehearted Commitment

◆ *Clean house of all false gods.*

God's first command was that His people were to worship no other gods (Exodus 20:3). Asa took his commitment to God seriously. First, he smashed up, cut down, and hauled off everything his people used to worship false gods (2 Chronicles 14:3). As I mentioned before, he even went so far as to remove his own grandmother as Queen Mother because she had made a pole for the worship of the false god Asherah (15:16–19).

You cannot be sold out to God and to other gods at the same time. The God-shaped void in your heart has room for only one god—the true God.

Jesus said that we cannot serve two masters (Matthew 6:24), nor can we love both God and Money (Matthew 6:24). He said that we needed to put God ahead of our family (Luke 14:26), ourselves (Luke 14:26), and everything else (Luke 14:33). When we put Him first, He makes everything else better (Matthew 6:33).

God does not manifest His presence through the lives of those with crowded hearts. His presence is released when He finds hearts totally committed to Him, first and foremost. What do you tend to put ahead of God?

◆ *Seek God.*

Asa not only got rid of the false gods but he also pursued the true One. The God-shaped void had been emptied of false gods and was then filled with the real God. The people of Judah gave themselves to seek the Lord, and He was found by them. What a treasure!

> "The LORD is with you when you are with him. If you seek him, he will be found by you" (2 Chronicles 15:2).

◆ *Rely on God.*

Early in his life Asa was blessed because he relied on God when under attack (2 Chronicles 14:9–11). But at the end of his life he was rebuked because he failed to depend on God (16:8).

The greatest indicator of spiritual dependence is our prayer life. When we are depending on ourselves, we don't need to pray, so we don't. When we are relying on God, we cannot help but pray about everything.

What does your prayer life indicate about your commitment to God and your reliance on Him? Does it show that you are truly sold out to Him?

◆ *Make a covenant of total commitment.*

> They took an oath to the LORD with loud acclamation, with shouting and with trumpets and horns. All Judah rejoiced about the oath because they had sworn it wholeheartedly. They sought God eagerly, and he was found by them. (2 Chronicles 15:14–15)

Often a commitment is not real unless it goes public. The young man can say he loves the girl, but those are just words until he puts a ring on her finger and publicly says, "I do."

For students in our church, their commitment to God often becomes real when they stand in front of the church and make a pledge to God in the areas of maturity, ministry, and purity. My boys made that pledge, and it really caused them to step up for God. God drew near to help them.

Commitment is not dynamic until it is both specific and public. For me, commitment became authentic and powerful when I signed a blank contract with God and shared it publicly with others. The contract was very simple. Across the top I wrote, "God's Will." I left the body of it empty, for God to fill in as He wished. Then I signed and dated the bottom.

I remember the fearful joy that exploded in my chest when I signed my name on that piece of paper. I knew that God was watching and that we were both taking this very seriously. Sometime later I was sharing my testimony at a youth retreat. I held up my contract, explained it, and read it to them. At that moment I experienced the presence of God in a new, fresh, intimate, and powerful way. There was a noticeable hush in the audience as God moved in. Soon dozens of students rushed to the altar with their own handwritten contracts.

God's presence is released when we go public and get specific with our commitments to God.

What about you? Have you ever really "sold out" to God?

Have you ever given all that you know of yourself to all you know of God?

Have you put Him ahead of everything else?

Do you seriously seek Him?

Have you ever gone public with your commitment?

Will you do so now?

### God's Will

Name: _____

Date: _____

### CHAPTER TWELVE:

# Connected to the Power
## Dependent Prayer

OR MY WIFE'S FORTIETH BIRTHDAY we planned a huge surprise party at a local swimming pool/picnic area. Many of her friends helped as we prepared food and fun for two hundred people. A week before the big day everything was falling into place—except the weather. May in Ohio is notorious for sudden, soaking thunderstorms. Such an outburst would obviously ruin our outdoor plans.

In the days leading up to the big night, the weather reports consistently predicted a major storm to hit central Ohio the very night of her party. There was one person I knew who had a hotline to the Master of the weather. So I called Mom and asked her to pray.

Two hours before the party was scheduled to start the radar showed a huge front of violent storms moving directly for our town. I called Mom and asked if she had prayed. She calmly told me not to worry—she and the Lord had this covered.

People began to call to ask if the party was still on. I relayed Mom's message and took the boys to the swimming pool to set up. Soon everyone, including Mom and Dad, arrived to await Cathy's arrival. She showed up right on time, appearing surprised and happy about the party. It was a beautiful, dry night, and the celebration was a wonderful success.

When we got home, we turned on the weather report in time to hear the broadcaster talking about the inexplicable way the storm split in two and *bypassed* our town. While the towns on either side of us were pounded by the storm, we did not have even one raindrop. He said he had no explanation for why it happened. We just laughed.

Although she got a late start as a prayer warrior and was less than five feet tall, my mother became a little giant at the throne of God. Growing up in the Quaker tradition influenced her attitude about public prayer; I never heard her pray aloud during my growing-up years. But while I was at college she joined a ladies' prayer group, and out of that she developed a very simple yet astoundingly powerful prayer life.

Her ability to touch the heart of God in simple, trusting prayer became apparent. Eventually I started saying, "If it's important, I'll pray about it. But if it's *really* important, let's get Mom to pray about it."

Her simple, trusting prayers had other results too. There was a wonderful change in her personality as she became full of love and joy. Her marriage relationship, which had been distant for years, became unusually close as Mom and Dad began to pray together every day.

Her ministry touched so many people that her pastor began to call her "Saint Bert" (her name was Bertha, which she was not fond of), and no one objected. Her prayers also brought untold blessings to our own family. I believe Mom prayed my sister, Carol, back to her husband, to God, to church, and to her extended family. Carol, a dynamo in her own right, now has a dynamic ministry to many women through her prayer and Bible study group.

My mom demonstrated that it is not the eloquence of the prayer that touches God. It is the heart of simple trust that He cannot resist.

## Bad News

He lived in the unprecedented splendor of the royal palace of the richest kingdom on earth. Yet his people lived in ruin and rubble. He held one of the highest offices in the land, but his people squatted in squalor. And it broke his heart.

Nehemiah was the cupbearer to the most powerful man on the planet, Artaxerxes, the king of Persia. As cupbearer, Nehemiah was not only trusted to taste-test the king's food for poison but he also controlled access to the king's private quarters. He was one of a very few people who had the ear of the king, part of a small company who spoke with the king on a daily basis.

A few years earlier a band of Hebrews had been given permission to leave Persia, their place of exile, and return to Jerusalem. They had rebuilt much of the temple, and later another group joined them to help restore worship practices. But a recent expedition had just returned from Jerusalem with sad news. The city itself still lay in distress and ruin. The wall protecting the city was broken down, and the gates of the city were burned. As a result, the people lived in fear of their enemies and felt shame for their situation. The news shook Nehemiah so deeply that he slumped to the ground in tears, broken by grief.

If that was all Nehemiah did, the story would end there, and history would be greatly altered. Fortunately, it did not end there. Nehemiah turned his sorrow over the problems into prayer, and the Immanuel Factor kicked in powerfully.

In answer to Nehemiah's prayers, God miraculously paved the way for him not only to leave his post and go to Jerusalem but also receive the incredible amount of provisions needed for rebuilding the wall. But we'll get to that later.

## PRINCIPLES OF THE IMMANUEL FACTOR

### 1. The Immanuel Factor rests on those who get through to God in prayer.

The presence of God attends the prayers of His people. One is drawn to the other with passion and purpose, almost like a mating dance. A taste of God creates a thirst for His presence that inevitably leads to prayer. Dependent prayer attracts God's attention and draws a greater manifestation of His presence. More of His presence causes more prayer. And on the dance goes, until the unmistakable presence of God is manifested in full force.

A simple summary of Nehemiah's autobiography reveals that he was a man of profoundly dependent prayer. The book bearing his name is not only an awesome manual on the art of spiritual leadership but is also a primer on the primacy of prayer. In almost every chapter of the book of Nehemiah, prayer is central. At every hand and in every situation, Nehemiah turned his problems over to God in prayer.

The concern of his heart was eight hundred miles away from where he was living. His people lived in the midst of destruction and faced possible annihilation. To further complicate matters, Nehemiah answered to an unbeliever, who could quickly order the beheading of subordinates who upset him.

In order to carry out what God had placed on his heart, Nehemiah would need a three-year leave of absence and enough supplies to rebuild the wall around the entire city of Jerusalem. Before that could occur, a huge change had to happen in the heart of the man in authority! To march into the king's oval office and demand so much time off and the materials needed to rebuild the wall would be like signing his death warrant.

So Nehemiah prayed.

Nehemiah was a God-reliant leader. It was the mark of his leadership, the essence of his being, the secret of his success, and the key to his experience of the Immanuel Factor.

His prayer demonstrates the art of dependent prayer that releases God's presence. Nehemiah did not pray formalistic prayers. His simple request arose out of the issues at hand and the burdens of his heart.

> They said to me, "Those who survived the exile and are back in the province are in great trouble and disgrace. The wall of Jerusalem is broken down, and its gates have been burned with fire." When I heard these things, I sat down and wept. For some days I mourned and fasted and prayed before the God of heaven. (Nehemiah 1:3–4)

When he heard of the plight of his people, Nehemiah's first

response was to pray. Too often we pray after all else has failed. Nehemiah was a successful leader because he prayed first. And he kept praying.

Nehemiah did not pray once and quit. He brought his burden to God repeatedly. His crying out to God lasted several "days." We don't know how long he sought God. It was possibly weeks, maybe even months after he first heard about the plight of Jerusalem before God granted His prayer request. But we do know he was persistent and persevering.

> "O Lord, God of heaven . . . *let your ear be attentive and your eyes open to hear the prayer your servant is praying before you day and night for your servants*, the people of Israel" (Nehemiah 1:6, emphasis added).

### Moved More by Our Hurt Than Our Eloquence

Nehemiah was heartbroken, and his prayer was desperate. And God responded. That's what fathers do. This was graphically illustrated by Jim Redmond in the 1992 Barcelona Olympics. His son, Derek, a twenty-six-year-old runner, was favored to win the four-hundred-meter gold medal. Then tragedy struck.

Midway through the race, Jim saw his son fall to the track, writhing in pain. Derek had ripped his hamstring. Something snapped in Jim's heart. He jumped to his feet and headed for his son.

Down on the track Derek fought to his feet. Blinded with tears, he began hopping down the track on his good leg.

Fighting his way through the crowd, the coaches, and the medical attendants, Jim got to his son and said, "You don't have to do this."

"Yes, I do," Derek responded.

"Then we're going to finish this together."

And they did. Wrapping Derek's arm around his shoulder the father helped his son totter off toward the finish line. With the son's head buried in the father's shoulder, the two made it all the way to the end together.

The father did not respond to his son's eloquence or his

strength. He responded to his stubborn insistence and obvious dependence. And our heavenly Father does as well.[1]

### BACK TO NEHEMIAH

Nehemiah was not only persistent in prayer but he also skill-fully reminded God of the promise He had given Moses. God had predicted that His people would one day be scattered through disobedience, and they were. He also promised that they would be restored to their homeland through obedience. Because of this, Nehemiah was convinced that God would act on his behalf. He was certain that God would keep the promise He made to His people.

> "Remember the instruction you gave your servant Moses, saying, 'If you are unfaithful, I will scatter you among the nations, but if you return to me and obey my commands, then even if your exiled people are at the farthest horizon, I will gather them from there and bring them to the place I have chosen as a dwelling for my Name.' They are your servants and your people, whom you redeemed by your great strength and your mighty hand" (Nehemiah 1:8–10).

But Nehemiah doesn't stop here. He asks God for what he needs in terms of help as well.

> "O Lord, let your ear be attentive to the prayer of this your servant and to the prayer of your servants who delight in revering your name. *Give your servant success today by granting him favor in the presence of this man.*" I was cupbearer to the king. (Nehemiah 1:11, emphasis added)

Nehemiah was obviously familiar with the book of Genesis and with the prayer of Abraham's servant, "Give me success today" (Genesis 24:12). To this request Nehemiah added a specific petition. He told God exactly what was needed for success: "Give your servant success today *by granting him favor in the presence of this man.*" Nehemiah was planning to ask the king to send him off with his blessing to rebuild the walls. Beyond that, Nehemiah wanted the king to pay for it!

When was the last time you experienced a serious season of prayer? When did you pour your heart out to God and ask Him to meet your specific needs?

2. **The Immanuel Factor accompanies those who keep their prayer connection to God continuously open.**

> In the month of Nisan in the twentieth year of King Artaxerxes, when wine was brought for him, I took the wine and gave it to the king. I had not been sad in his presence before; so the king asked me, "Why does your face look so sad when you are not ill? This can be nothing but sadness of heart." I was very much afraid. (Nehemiah 2:1–2)

Of course he was afraid. It was a capital offense to appear in the king's presence with an unhappy face. Nehemiah had one ace up his sleeve, though—the manifest presence of God. So he waded in:

> I was very much afraid, but I said to the king, "May the king live forever! Why should my face not look sad when the city where my fathers are buried lies in ruins, and its gates have been destroyed by fire?" The king said to me, "What is it you want?" (Nehemiah 2:2–4).

This was the big moment. If he did not have the king's favor, asking such an outlandish request would be fatal. God had to come through. So Nehemiah reminded Him of his request.

> Then I prayed to the God of heaven, and I answered the king, "If it pleases the king and if your servant has found favor in his sight, let him send me to the city in Judah where my fathers are buried so that I can rebuild it" (Nehemiah 2:4–5).

I love the way Nehemiah recorded what happened. "Then I prayed to the God of heaven, and I answered the king. . . ." This was not a matter of dropping on his knees and offering an eloquent baritone invocation. It was a quick cry from out of his heart. Silent to man, it was nonetheless quite audible to God. It probably took less than a second, but it changed the rest of his life as well as the history of the Jewish nation.

### An Unending Conversation With God

One of the most wonderful results of committing my life to God was the discovery of a sensational "secret friend." My sister went to college when I was six, and my brother was married when I was eleven. So I often felt lonely around the house. But my relationship with God meant that I was never really alone. He was available all day long. So I talked with Him.

Such simple ongoing dialogue with God was a key aspect of Nehemiah's prayer life. It is also a key to releasing the manifest presence of God.

We don't know *what* Nehemiah prayed; we just know *that* he prayed. It might have been "Help," or "Here we go," or "This is it," or "Now is the time." When crunch time came, Nehemiah met it with prayer.

When I was a high school wrestler, I used to be scared. I was scared of losing, afraid of letting down my team, and worried about getting hurt. One night before a match I read 2 Timothy 1:7 (NKJV): "For God has not given us a spirit of fear, but of power and of love and of a sound mind."

I thought, *That is exactly what I need. I need God's Spirit to overcome my fear by giving me power to do my best; I need love to help me witness to my opponent after the match, and a sound mind so that I don't get rattled and make a costly mistake.*

When I walked out on the mat for the match and shook my opponent's hand, I breathed to God a simple, dependent prayer, *"No fear, but love, power, and a sound mind."* As I did so, a divine calm settled over me just as the referee blew the whistle. I wrestled the best match of my life that day and won easily. The "no fear" prayer became my mute mantra from then on. I didn't always win the match, but I did find the freedom to do my best as God's presence supplied me with His power, His love, and His awesome peace.

3. **The Immanuel Factor resides on those who are God-dependent on the inside while active on the outside.**

Nehemiah stands out as an exceptionally effective spiritual leader, because the entire time he was leading in his outer life he was communing with God in his interior life. It is the essence of praying "without ceasing" (1 Thessalonians 5:17 NKJV).

### A SANCTUARY OF THE SOUL

Born in 1893, Thomas Kelly grew up in a Quaker community near my hometown in Ohio. As a college student, Thomas once said to a professor, "I am going to make my life a miracle." And from then on he set impossibly high standards for his life. He labored continuously to become a successful pastor, scholar, and professor. But by the age of forty-three, his endless efforts had driven him to exhaustion.

It is often at our lowest point that we experience our deepest intimacy with God. Kelly shifted his focus from acquiring more knowledge *about* God to developing his relationship *with* God. At this point he discovered something peaceful, wonderful, and powerful. He referred to it as a sanctuary of the soul. In his classic work *A Testament of Devotion*, Kelly wrote,

> Deep within us all there is an amazing inner sanctuary of the soul, a holy place, a Divine Center, a speaking voice to which we may continuously return. Eternity is at our hearts, pressing upon our time-torn lives, warming us with intimations of astounding destiny, calling us home unto Itself. . . . It is the Shekinah of the soul, the Presence in the midst.[2]

Kelly found that the sanctuary of God's presence brought unhurried serenity, peace, and power in the midst of the hustle of life. He saw the key to the sanctuary as simple prayer. He taught through coaching that the art of simple prayer was consistently turning our thoughts to God.

> What is urged are secret habits of unceasing orientation of the depths of our being. . . . so we are perpetually bowed in worship while we are very busy in the world of daily

affairs. What is urged are inward practices of the mind at the deepest levels, letting it swing like a needle to the polestar of the soul.[3]

Like me, you may ask, "How can I get my heart to *continually* turn to God?" Fortunately, Kelly has advice for that.

How? By quiet, persistent practice in turning all of our being, day and night, in prayer and inward worship and surrender, toward him who calls in the deeps of our souls. Mental habits of inward orientation must be established. An inner, secret turning to God can be made fairly steady, after weeks and months and years of practice and lapses and failures and returns.[4]

### Too Busy Not to Pray

I am only an apprentice in the deeper life and the art of contemplation. As such, I am a big fan of silence and solitude as super aids in building a familiar friendship with God. However, as the parent of high school students and a pastor who oversees thirty-five employees, I know that silence and solitude are hard to come by. And I also know that if I think I have a challenge developing my interior life, how much more does the mother of preschoolers or the single working mom feel the challenge?

Nehemiah was an officer in the inner circle of the king of the most powerful nation on earth in his day. His life also would have had its fair share of hectic moments. Yet he learned to take his quiet time with God into his noisy times of the day—through simple prayer. Right in the middle of his conversation with the king he was talking with God in prayer. His mouth and body were engaged in dialogue with the king while his mind and spirit were in contact with the King of Kings.

Simple, dependent, ongoing dialogue with God was a key aspect of Nehemiah's prayer life. It is also a key to releasing the manifest presence of God. When God is present, everything is better. So when we go through the day continually inviting God to intervene, He adds His value to everything we do.

## 4. God cannot resist sincerely dependent prayer.

Nehemiah's fate, as well as the fate of the Israelites living in Jerusalem, rested on the response of the king. But when Nehemiah prayed and plunged ahead with his petition, he was not alone. God was with him. And "God with us" makes all the difference.

> Then the king, with the queen sitting beside him, asked me, "How long will your journey take, and when will you get back?" It pleased the king to send me; so I set a time. (Nehemiah 2:6)

"It pleased the king to send me." That's it. Unbelievable, impossible, amazing! God came through. Nehemiah sensed he was on a roll. So instead of quitting while he was ahead, Nehemiah pressed on.

> I also said to him, "If it pleases the king, may I have letters to the governors of Trans-Euphrates, so that they will provide me safe-conduct until I arrive in Judah? And may I have a letter to Asaph, keeper of the king's forest, so he will give me timber to make beams for the gates of the citadel by the temple and for the city wall and for the residence I will occupy?" (Nehemiah 2:7–8).

First, God moved so that the king would allow him to go. Now Nehemiah was asking the king to pay for safe conduct and supplies. Did he go too far? No. He was in the midst of the Immanuel Factor, and he felt it wise to ask for the help and supplies he needed to get the job done.

> And *because the gracious hand of my God was upon me*, the king granted my requests. So I went to the governors of Trans-Euphrates and gave them the king's letters. The king had also sent army officers and cavalry with me. (Nehemiah 2:8–9, emphasis added)

God was with him. As a result of God's manifest presence, the king gave Nehemiah all he had asked for *plus* an army/cavalry escort!

## How to Release the Presence of God Through Dependent Prayer

◆ *Develop a regular appointment where you can pour your heart out to God.*

As I already mentioned in chapter 2, it is important to schedule a time, preferably the same time every day, to meet with God. Try to meet Him in the same place. Have a plan of how you'll spend your time with God.

My current plan involves three disciplines: Bible reading, journaling, and prayer. First, I read the Bible till God speaks to me. Usually it's a chapter or two through a book of the Bible. I alternate between reading a book of the Old Testament and a book of the New Testament. Then I journal, focusing on the events of the last day and those planned for the coming day. Then I turn them into prayer. Continuing my prayer time, I use a few lists to help me pray consistently for the needs of others.

Your scheduled time with God will probably look different than mine. The point I'm making here is to make sure that we connect with God *before* facing the challenges of our day.

### What Is Your Excuse?

One woman who had every excuse to neglect daily time with God was Susanna Wesley. In nineteen years she gave birth to nineteen children, nine of whom died as infants—including two sets of twins. One baby was accidentally smothered by a maid. Another was crippled for life in a tragic accident.

Susanna homeschooled her children and was the key person for fostering spiritual development in each of their lives. She scheduled a private appointment with each child once a week. These bonds of faith and love helped them survive continual hardships.

Her husband, Samuel, was a poor pastor and an ineffective manager of money. Despite his love for her and his commitment to Christ, Samuel was blind to his faults. At times he was tyrannical and despotic at home. Once after a minor disagreement, he abandoned Susanna and their many children *for an entire year* while pursuing another ministry.

During the year of his absence, Susanna decided to hold Sunday evening church in her home for her children. Amazingly, this meeting quickly grew to between two and three hundred people!

In all of the hectic seasons of her life, Susanna still made time to meet with God, usually for an hour each day. When she needed some stillness, she would throw her apron up over her head. Her children were trained to let her alone during that time.[5]

Not one, but two of Susanna's sons, John and Charles Wesley, were key players in the Great Awakening that swept England and the United States in the mid–1700s. They traced their ability to connect with God and release His presence in dependent prayer back to their mother.

◆ *Learn to take your quiet time into your noisy life by practicing the art of simple prayer.*

Silently talk to God all day long. Breathe out one-word prayers, such as "Help," "Wisdom," "Thanks," or "Forgive" as fits the situation. The goal is to stay connected to God all day long.

Prayer is the lifeline of the person living in the Immanuel Factor. Without that open channel and constant communion, the presence of God evaporates from our lives. Let me encourage you to give God a prime piece of your time each day, and then try to keep the communion going all day long. Learn to cultivate His presence through continual communion.

### CHAPTER THIRTEEN:

# Jumpin' Jehoshaphat
## Praise Warfare

---

*"Praise is our official invitation for Jesus to take charge of the situation."*

—DON MCMINN[1]

---

AFTER HE GOT OFF THE PHONE, my friend Jack was stunned and shocked. After years of prayers and tears, his troubled seventeen-year-old son, Jesse, had taken his life. For Jack, the next few days, filled with preparations, the funeral, and the burial, were a numb blur of silent misery. Doubtful, despairing, even demonic thoughts flooded his mind and assailed his soul.

The day after the burial he was driving out to the grave site alone in his wife's van. Unconsciously Jack mumbled, "God, I'm hurting. I need something." Then he punched on the tape player.

But the words of the praise song on the tape made his blood boil.

"Celebrate Jesus, celebrate!"

Jack began to pound the dash and steering wheel of the van in a bitter rage. A torrent of venomous resentment poured out of his broken heart as he lashed out at the God he refused to celebrate. *"How can I celebrate a God who lets this happen to my son?"* he raged. Then the second song on the tape began.

"Jesus, lover of my soul.

Jesus, you will never let me go."

"At that moment," Jack said, "I felt God wrapping His arms around me and pulling me so close I couldn't pound on Him anymore. I was so wrapped up in God's love that all I could do was cry."

Through this experience Jack learned the power of praise warfare. And so can you. A man named Jehoshaphat will be our guide.

## A Great Start Led to Great Blessing

Jehoshaphat succeeded his father, Asa, as king of Judah. He followed his father's commitment to the Lord and experienced the blessings of the Immanuel Factor as a result.

> *The LORD was with Jehoshaphat* because in his early years he walked in the ways his father David had followed. He did not consult the Baals but sought the God of his father and followed his commands rather than the practices of Israel. The LORD established the kingdom under his control; and all Judah brought gifts to Jehoshaphat, so that he had great wealth and honor. (2 Chronicles 17:3–5, emphasis added)

Jehoshaphat was not content expressing his father's level of dedication to the Lord; he took initiatives to lead his entire nation to a greater commitment to the Lord. He even sent his officials and priests throughout the land to teach the people the ways of God. The level of God's manifest presence was so increased in Judah that their aggressive neighboring nations took notice and kept their distance. Some even brought tribute to Jehoshaphat, and he became a highly honored and wealthy king.

## Poor Choices Led to Near Disaster

Like most of us, Jehoshaphat allowed prosperity to become a greater challenge to him than adversity had been. Even though he was being blessed mightily by the Immanuel Factor at work in his life and should have known better, Jehoshaphat made a political alliance with his greatest rival—Ahab, the wicked king of Israel. What was he thinking? As long as Jehoshaphat had God's presence he didn't need an alliance with Ahab.

This compromising decision soon brought trouble to Judah; Ahab asked Jehoshaphat to join forces with him to fight Ahab's enemy, Syria.

To his credit, Jehoshaphat would not go forward without encouraging Ahab to first consult the Lord. But Ahab's advisors were as ungodly as he was. Their counsel could not be trusted. When a godly counselor was found in Ahab's kingdom, Ahab threw him into prison for predicting Ahab's downfall and death in the coming battle. Jehoshaphat should never have aligned his nation with such a wicked ruler. This was abundantly clear from the outset.

When the battle began, Ahab hid in a disguise and set Jehoshaphat up as a target to be killed by the enemy. But God was still with Jehoshaphat and not with Ahab. When Jehoshaphat was mistaken for Ahab by the Syrians and became the object of their attack, he cried out to the Lord, and He diverted the enemy away. About the same time, an archer's random shot caught Ahab between the joints of his armor and killed him! With God's protection Jehoshaphat escaped injury.

### Leadership With Integrity Led to Greater Prosperity

Jehoshaphat learned his lesson about the dangers of compromise. So he set about deepening the reforms he had previously begun. He started by working to get his nation on the right page.

> Jehoshaphat lived in Jerusalem, and he went out again among the people from Beersheba to the hill country of Ephraim and turned them back to the LORD, the God of their fathers. He appointed judges in the land, in each of the fortified cities of Judah. He told them, "Consider carefully what you do, because you are not judging for man but for the LORD, who is with you whenever you give a verdict. Now let the fear of the LORD be upon you. Judge carefully, for with the LORD our God there is no injustice or partiality or bribery" (2 Chronicles 19:4–7).

Then he turned his attention to the officials in the capital of Jerusalem.

> In Jerusalem also, Jehoshaphat appointed some of the Levites, priests and heads of Israelite families to administer the law of the LORD and to settle disputes. And they lived in Jerusalem. He gave them these orders: "You must serve faithfully and wholeheartedly in the fear of the LORD. In every case that comes before you from your fellow countrymen who live in the cities—whether bloodshed or other concerns of the law, commands, decrees or ordinances—you are to warn them not to sin against the LORD; otherwise his wrath will come on you and your brothers. Do this, and you will not sin. . . . Act with courage, and may the LORD be with those who do well" (2 Chronicles 19:8–11).

Later in his reign, Jehoshaphat faced an impossible situation. A threefold alliance of nations—the Moabites, the Ammonites, and the Meunites—banded together to try to oust Jehoshaphat. Their massive combined forces marched north from the Dead Sea through a mountain pass and were approaching Jerusalem before Jehoshaphat could do anything about it. To his credit, he took five decisive steps that prepared the way for a miraculous release of the manifest presence of God on his nation's behalf. Each gives us greater insight into the presence of God. They build upon one another to light the fuse for the explosive power of praise warfare.

### PRINCIPLES OF THE IMMANUEL FACTOR

1. **The presence of God is nurtured as a result of corporately seeking God through prayer and fasting.**

> Alarmed, Jehoshaphat resolved to inquire of the LORD, and he proclaimed a fast for all Judah. The people of Judah came together to seek help from the LORD; indeed, they came from every town in Judah to seek him. (2 Chronicles 20:3–4)

When faced with a crisis, Jehoshaphat turned to God in earnest. As we saw with Moses, prayer and fasting have a way of purifying our hearts, clarifying our focus, and raising our sensitivity to the personal presence of God. The difference is that Moses sought God individually, while Jehoshaphat rallied his whole nation to seek God.

There is great power when many people seek after God together (Matthew 18:20). If Jesus shows up when two or three gather in His name, imagine the effect when thousands fast and pray together! At our church, we usually set aside a week or two each year for collective prayer and fasting. Some of our best times in the Lord have come as a result of seeking God in this way.

## 2. The manifest presence of God is cultivated when we remind God of His promises.

Jehoshaphat didn't just pray—he prayed with great passion and wisdom. Standing in the temple courts, Jehoshaphat reminded God of the promises made there when the temple was constructed.

> "O LORD, God of our fathers, are you not the God who is in heaven? You rule over all the kingdoms of the nations. Power and might are in your hand, and no one can withstand you. O our God, did you not drive out the inhabitants of this land before your people Israel and give it forever to the descendants of Abraham your friend? They have lived in it and have built in it a sanctuary for your Name, saying, 'If calamity comes upon us, whether the sword of judgment, or plague or famine, we will stand in your presence before this temple that bears your Name and will cry out to you in our distress, and you will hear us and save us'" (2 Chronicles 20:6–9).

There are hundreds of promises in the Bible, one for every need. A study of the great prayer warriors in the Bible reveals the power of reminding God of His promises. It brings authority to the situation. In a sense, it puts God in a situation where He has a greater obligation to respond.

Every three months I take a promise from the Word that seems to speak to my situation. Then I focus my personal petitions on that promise. I ask God to make it real in my circumstances and to do "exceeding abundantly above all" I can "ask or think" (Ephesians 3:20 KJV) regarding that promise in my life. And such praying makes a difference.

### 3. The manifest presence of God comes when we get desperate before God.

It is not easy for anyone to admit weakness and helplessness. It is especially hard for a king to confess that he has no idea what to do. But Jehoshaphat did just that, and it paid off.

> "O our God, will you not judge them? For we have no power to face this vast army that is attacking us. We do not know what to do, but our eyes are upon you" (2 Chronicles 20:12).

The Father-heart of God cannot help but be touched by the desperate cries of His children. When we depend on ourselves, He will usually back off and let us handle it. But when all of our reliance is fixed totally on Him, we can be sure that He will respond.

God is wiser than any of us and bigger than any problem we have. When we stop looking to ourselves for the solution and start looking to God, we are often on our way to a miracle. That's what happened to Jehoshaphat.

### 4. The manifest presence of God is available when we believe God's Word.

When Jehoshaphat and the people of Judah got serious about seeking God, He responded. He prompted Jahaziel, one of the priestly prophets, to give Jehoshaphat and company a very encouraging word.

> "This is what the LORD says to you: 'Do not be afraid or discouraged because of this vast army. For the battle is not

yours, but God's. Tomorrow march down against them. They will be climbing up by the Pass of Ziz, and you will find them at the end of the gorge in the Desert of Jeruel. You will not have to fight this battle. Take up your positions; stand firm and see the deliverance the LORD will give you, O Judah and Jerusalem. Do not be afraid; do not be discouraged. Go out to face them tomorrow, and the LORD will be with you'" (2 Chronicles 20:15–17).

If I got this word from God, I would be tempted to say, "Are you sure? Let me get this straight. We are to march into battle, but not fight? You have got to be kidding!" But Jehoshaphat didn't. He believed the word of God and counted on the presence of God to be with them and to be enough. God promised to be with them, and that was all he needed.

> Jehoshaphat stood and said, "Listen to me, Judah and people of Jerusalem! Have faith in the LORD your God and you will be upheld; have faith in his prophets and you will be successful" (2 Chronicles 20:20).

Faith in faith accomplishes nothing. Faith in the wrong thing can be deadly. But faith in the Word of God sets the table for the active discharge of the power of God into the situation.

## 5. The manifest presence of God is detonated by praise warfare.

Along with the Joshua-plan to march around the city seven times and blow trumpets, Jehoshaphat's strategy ranks as one of the most bizarre, risky, and ultimately successful battle plans in all of history. It was strange: Face the enemy with praise and thanksgiving. It was simple: All he did was line up the singing priests to lead the way into battle. That's it! His only weapon was *praise*. Not chariots, not swords, not archers, not cavalry, just singers. Praise warfare. It was insane. It was also brilliant.

> Jehoshaphat appointed men to sing to the LORD and to praise him for the splendor of his holiness as they went out at the head of the army, saying: "Give thanks to the LORD, for his love endures forever" (2 Chronicles 20:21).

I am eager to get to heaven, walk into the "You Were There" theater, and see the video of this battle. I want to see the looks on the faces of Jehoshaphat's enemies. They were preparing to march to battle against an army of priests whose only visible weapon was a song. They must have licked their chops, thinking it would be a slaughter. And it was.

> As they began to sing and praise, the LORD set ambushes against the men of Ammon and Moab and Mount Seir who were invading Judah, and they were defeated. The men of Ammon and Moab rose up against the men from Mount Seir to destroy and annihilate them. After they finished slaughtering the men from Seir, they helped to destroy one another. When the men of Judah came to the place that overlooks the desert and looked toward the vast army, they saw only dead bodies lying on the ground; no one had escaped. (2 Chronicles 20:22–24)

What a fantastic scene! Jehoshaphat's army marched south with a hastily gathered group led by some praising priests. The enemy was just over the hill. They crested the knoll and were stunned by what they saw. Before them was an ocean of carnage. Thousands of corpses dressed for battle were scattered across the field. It was a slaughter all right; none of the enemy remained.

A key word in this story is the tiny word *as*. God did not fight for them *before* they praised. He fought for them *as* they praised. Their praise released the manifest presence of God to totally defeat their enemies. After that, all Jehoshaphat's army needed to do was to pick up the spoils. This turned out to be a much larger task for them than fighting the battle, because gathering the plunder took three days (2 Chronicles 20:25).

Praise warfare was one of the most effective weapons of mass destruction ever employed. It wiped out three armies. It produced three days of spoils. It was amazing. The reason for the results was not the beauty of the singers' wardrobes or the strength of their voices. There was no magic in the words of their song. The power came from the dramatic discharge of the manifest presence of God that was released by their praise.

### PRAISE SETS THE CAPTIVE FREE

Wesley Duewel has written several powerful books about prayer and revival. In his book *Mighty Prevailing Prayer*, he tells of the power of praise to set a captive free:

> During my missionary days in India, students and staff of the girls' Bible school of another society were praying and fasting for a demon-possessed student to be delivered. I was called to help, but felt so helpless. As I prayed, I was impressed to go to the struggling, semiconscious girl being held down by several adults as they tried to control her thrashing and jerking.
>
> I called into her ear, "Jai, Masih Ki" (victory to Christ), the idiomatic way to say, "Praise the Lord" in her language. As I called this sentence into her ear, she began to respond as if she could hear what I was saying. Then she struggled to control her locked mouth, and when she finally forced it open, called out after me, "Jai Masih Ki." Instantly, she was delivered. Prayer and fasting probably helped prepare the way, but praise was the Spirit's weapon to set her free.[2]

### ALL SHOOK UP

Praise warfare has the power to detonate an explosion of the presence of God. Once a pair of missionaries, a jailer, and a jail full of other prisoners felt its mighty power.

Paul and Silas arrived in Philippi, hoping to plant a church. Instead, they found themselves in prison. They had cast a demon out of a fortune-telling slave girl. Unfortunately, the girl's owners did not appreciate the potential lost income; they stirred up the crowd and the authorities against Paul and Silas. So the missionaries were severely beaten and taken to the inner cell of the prison where their feet were locked in stocks.

I don't know what you would do in that situation, but I'd have a tendency toward self-pity. Such a rotten time would lead me to pout and whine—but not Paul and Silas. They chose to praise and worship instead. The Bible puts it this way: "About midnight Paul and Silas were praying and singing hymns to God, and the other prisoners were listening to them" (Acts 16:25).

We do not know what hymns they sang to God, although there is one song repeated throughout the Old Testament. It is found in Psalm 118. It also just happened to be the same song sung by the priests of Jehoshaphat. When you see how appropriate the words of this psalm are to their plight, it is easy to imagine Paul and Silas regaling God and the other prisoners with this song.

> Give thanks to the LORD, for He is good; His love endures forever. In my anguish I cried to the LORD, and he answered by setting me free. The LORD is with me; I will not be afraid. What can man do to me? The LORD is with me; He is my helper. I will look in triumph on my enemies. It is better to take refuge in the LORD than to trust in man. It is better to take refuge in the LORD than to trust in princes. The LORD is my strength and my song; he has become my salvation. I will not die but live, and will proclaim what the LORD has done. This is the day the Lord has made; let us rejoice and be glad in it. O LORD, save us; O LORD, grant us success. You are my God, and I will give you thanks; you are my God, and I will exalt you. Give thanks to the LORD, for he is good; his love endures forever. (Psalm 118:1, 5–9, 14, 17, 24–25, 28–29)

God obviously heard and enjoyed their singing prayer of praise and worship.

> Suddenly there was such a violent earthquake that the foundations of the prison were shaken. At once all the prison doors flew open, and everybody's chains came loose. The jailer woke up, and when he saw the prison doors open, he drew his sword and was about to kill himself because he thought the prisoners had escaped. But Paul shouted, "Don't harm yourself! We are all here!" The jailer called for lights, rushed in and fell trembling before Paul and Silas. He then brought them out and asked, "Sirs, what must I do to be saved?" (Acts 16:26–30).

Praise warfare not only released the power of God to set Paul and Silas free from their bonds but it also set the jailer and his family free from sin. Never underestimate the power of praise warfare!

## Praise and Worship Warfare

◆ *Praise allows us to enter the presence of God.*

The psalmist wrote,

> Enter his gates with thanksgiving and his courts with praise; give thanks to him and praise his name. (Psalm 100:4)
> But You are holy, enthroned in the praises of Israel. (Psalm 22:3 NKJV)

◆ *It takes faith to practice praise warfare.*

Praise that is offered as a result of blessing, and after the crisis is over, is expected. Praise that is offered *before* the blessing, and *in the midst* of the crisis, is both rare and explosive. It is an act of faith. As such, it is like pulling the pin on a grenade. It detonates the presence of God to explode on the scene.

Bible teacher Watchman Nee expressed it this way:

> There is power in praise which prayer does not have. Of course, the distinction between the two is artificial. . . . The highest expression of faith is not prayer in its ordinary sense of petition, but prayer in its sublimest expression of praise.[3]

◆ *You won't be able to offer praise in the heat of battle if you haven't learned to do so in peacetime.*

Jehoshaphat had learned to pursue God at the feet of his father. He had sent the priests throughout the land to teach the people to walk with God. When they faced the enemy in 2 Chronicles 20, it was not the first time they had sought God by giving Him praise. They had practiced this so much that it had become a habit. Therefore, when the battle plan was given, praise flowed naturally.

Paul and Silas were not rookies in the school of praise either. Paul's passion in life was to know God and to make Him known. His letters are filled with deep veins that are rich in praise. When the impossible came, he only knew one response—singing praises to God.

◆ *Praise warfare, like light, powerfully dispels the darkness.*

I spent two summers doing street ministry in Manhattan. We shared our lodging with a heavy cockroach population. We did not see them during the day, but they came out at night. When the lights were turned on you could hear them scatter.

Often when I am in church and the praise is flowing, I picture demons fleeing our premises like those roaches fled the light. Demons can't stand to be where God is being praised.

Watchmen Nee wrote, "Do remember: whenever God's children are praising, Satan must flee. Prayer frequently is a battle, but praise is victory. Prayer is spiritual warfare, but praise is the shout of triumph. For this reason praise is that which Satan hates most."[4]

◆ *Praise warfare may lead to the sacrifice of the immediate for the greater good of the eternal.*

The stories I recounted of Jack, Jehoshaphat, and Paul and Silas reveal the awesome power of praise warfare to affect present outcomes. But we need to remember that God deserves praise whether we get anything out of it or not. We also need to understand that praise releases the presence of God to work in His way for His *eternal* glory.

Fifty years ago Jim Elliot and a band of four other missionaries set out to take the good news of Jesus to the Auca tribe in Ecuador. His prayer was, "Oh, for a faith that sings! Father, I want to sing over the Aucas."

After arriving they sang a hymn of praise:

"We rest on Thee, Our Shield and our Defender.
Thine is the battle, Thine shall be the praise.
When passing through the gates of pearly splendor,
Victors, we rest with Thee through countless days."

The missionaries tried to make friends with the Aucas. In spite of their best efforts, however, the suspicious Indians killed them all and left their bodies on the beach. The tragedy was carried as the cover story of national newspapers in the United States. Amazingly, some of the men's relatives (including Jim Elliot's wife, Elisabeth) later returned to work with the Aucas. And even more amazingly, many of the Aucas in time came to trust Christ.

When asked to describe the events surrounding the death of the five missionaries, the Aucas recounted a bizarre scene. After the men were killed, singing was heard and a host of "people" was seen above the trees. They were all singing and holding hundreds of bright lights. Angels must have been ushering the missionaries through the gates of splendor. So Jim did get to sing over the Aucas, in answer to his prayer.[5]

Let me encourage you to become a praise warrior. You may not feel especially gifted or talented to do great things for God, but if you learn to respond to tough situations with praise, God will do great things for you . . . just like He did for Jehoshaphat.

CHAPTER FOURTEEN:

# God Pleasers
## *Gratifying God*

A S I WRITE THIS CHAPTER, it is beginning to feel a lot like
Christmas. Cheerful Christmas carols ring out from the
piano. Outside the window of my study, snowflakes flutter in the
air and white Christmas lights twinkle. Just across the hall, a
warm and inviting light from the carefully decorated Christmas
tree floods the living room. The smell of hot chocolate wafts
temptingly through the house.

My old Bible is opened to Luke's gospel—the familiar story
of the angel's visit to the Virgin Mary. How often we miss the
significant in the midst of the familiar. As my eyes slowly scan
the passage, I hear the words in my head of the well-known
account. Then five words jump out, and the whole story takes
on new significance.

> And in the sixth month the angel Gabriel was sent from
> God unto a city of Galilee, named Nazareth, to a virgin
> espoused to a man whose name was Joseph, of the house of
> David; and the virgin's name was Mary. And the angel came
> in unto her, and said, Hail, thou that art highly favoured, *the
> Lord is with thee:* blessed art thou among women. (Luke
> 1:26–28 KJV, emphasis added)

Did you notice the five often overlooked words? "The Lord
is with thee." Mary lived in the Immanuel Factor! If this were
merely a greeting, Gabriel would have said, "May the Lord be

with thee." But he was making an observation. God was *already* with her. Mary was a person who lived in the manifest presence of God.

You know the rest of the story. Gabriel explained to her that she was going to have a baby, the Son of God! She, of course, had some trouble understanding how this could happen, since she was a virgin. Gabriel explained that God was going to work a miracle in her womb, and Mary replied by saying she was willing for all of that to happen.

Later Mary went to visit her cousin Elizabeth, who was also carrying a baby, after many years of barrenness. They rejoiced at their amazing good fortune. Then Mary launched into a beautiful sonnet on the wonderful works of God, in both her life and throughout the ages.

Joseph took her to Bethlehem, where she delivered the miracle baby in a barn. Shepherds and wise men visited Jesus, and Mary struggled to grasp the significance of what was occurring. Later she and Joseph produced several children of their own.

Jesus left the carpenter trade at the age of thirty and spent three and a half years doing a whirlwind ministry. Then He was brutally executed as Mary helplessly watched. Three days later He rose from the dead, and forty days after that He ascended into heaven. The next week Mary, along with many others, prayed down the day of Pentecost, and the church was born. After that, this precious woman fades from the Scriptures.

Our journey to understanding the manifest presence of God leads us back to when Mary is first introduced to us. In Luke's record, we learn two primary truths about the Immanuel Factor.

## PRINCIPLES OF THE IMMANUEL FACTOR

### 1. God's presence adorns those who please Him. (Luke 1:28)

God's presence clung to Mary like an expensive perfume, but some might wonder why. What was it that drew the manifest presence of God to a teenage girl? What was it about her that caused Gabriel to immediately exclaim, "The Lord is with you"?

A closer look at the passage reveals the answer.

> One month later God sent the angel Gabriel to the town of Nazareth in Galilee with a message for a virgin named Mary. She was engaged to Joseph from the family of King David. The angel greeted Mary and said, "You are truly blessed! *The Lord is with you.*" Mary was confused by the angel's words and wondered what they meant. Then the angel told Mary, "Don't be afraid! God is pleased with you" (Luke 1:26–30 CEV, emphasis added).

God's presence clung to Mary like sweet incense *because* He was pleased with her. She made Him happy. Looking at Mary brought a smile to His face.

People hang out with the people they like. God is a person, and He hangs out most with the people He likes the most. Yes, He loves all of us unconditionally, but He does not manifest His presence unconditionally. He manifests His presence with those who please Him.

Every time the Bible records an angel appearing to a human, the angel says, "Don't be afraid!" I guess the sight of an angel is pretty intimidating. Yet even though they always say, "Don't be afraid!" they don't always say, "The Lord is with you" or "The Lord is pleased with you." They can't. This is because not every person an angel appeared to was a person experiencing the Immanuel Factor. But Mary did—God was pleased with her.

God is pleased with those who seek Him, but He is especially blessed by God *pleasers* like Mary.

I would like to think that if an angel appeared to me, the angel would say, "The Lord is with you" and "The Lord is pleased with you." But I know, and regret, that there are times when that would not be the case.

## 2. God is most pleased with us when we are most pleased in Him.

After visiting with her cousin Elizabeth and discussing the astonishing events they were experiencing as miracle mothers-to-be, Mary unleashed a glorious cry of praise to God. A careful study of her praise reveals a girl who had a Scripture-saturated mind and a holy heart. Her supreme source of joy was in God, not in other things.

Even though her fiancé, Joseph, had obviously captured a piece of her heart, his name surprisingly does not even appear in the thirty-some verses (Luke 1:26–56) that describe her encounter with Gabriel, informing Mary of her coming pregnancy. Even though a wedding loomed on the horizon, it does not seem to be dominating her mind. Her words are saturated with references to God, but there are none about Joseph. In talking with the angel, she doesn't even ask, "What will Joseph think? Or my parents? Or my friends?"

She loved God more than she loved her fiancé, more than her parents, more than her friends, more than her wedding, and most important, more than herself. She truly loved God with all of her heart, soul, mind, and strength. She sought first His kingdom and His righteousness. And when God found a girl with such a heart, He loved to be with her, selecting her to be the mother of His Son.

### How Mary Pleased God

Mary embodied all that pleases God. From her we see several keys to delighting His heart.

#### BE PURE BEFORE GOD (LUKE 1:27, 34)

Mary was a virgin. She had kept herself sexually pure. It might not have been easy. Her hometown of Nazareth was not a godly place. Many Roman soldiers were stationed there. It was a town with a reputation.

Later in Jesus' life the lie the enemy spread about Him was that He was the product of an illicit union between Mary and a Roman soldier. The fact that she was a virgin must not be overlooked or undervalued. She was pure in body, but this was merely a reflection of the fact that she was pure in heart.

Jesus taught that purity of heart was a requirement and a doorway into the presence of God: "Blessed are the pure in heart, for they will see God" (Matthew 5:8).

Being pure in heart means two things. First, it is having a heart that is unpolluted by sin. A pure heart is not dirtied by sin. Sin is avoided or quickly and thoroughly confessed and forsaken.

Second, a pure heart is undiluted. It has no foreign substances. When something is 100 percent pure, it means there are no additives. When a heart is pure, nothing—not even good things—takes God's place in the center of our affections. A pure heart is an uncluttered heart.

Having a pure heart is essential to experiencing the presence of God. In reference to the presence of God, David asked, "Who may ascend the hill of the LORD? Who may stand in his holy place?" (Psalm 24:3).

The answer is, "He who has clean hands and a *pure heart*, who does not lift up his soul to an idol or swear by what is false" (Psalm 24:4, emphasis added).

Later, after his sin with Bathsheba, one prayer filled David's heart: "Create in me a pure heart, O God, and renew a steadfast spirit within me" (Psalm 51:10).

When David dealt with his heart and confessed his sin, his heart was made pure again. Then God's presence returned. God is pleased with those who live to please Him. When we are pure in heart, like Mary, we are especially pleasing to God.

### SUBMIT TO GOD (LUKE 1:38)

Imagine: Out of the blue, the angel Gabriel appeared to an unknown virgin and told her she was going to have a baby. This divine interruption would change all of her plans. Getting pregnant like this would jeopardize her relationship with Joseph, her upcoming wedding and marriage, and potentially her life. After all, the baby in her womb was not just any baby; the child she would deliver was going to be the Son of God.

Yet Mary's heart was submissive to God. It was like wet clay in the hands of a potter. Her life was a blank contract before Him. So with absolutely no thought of her will, her way, or her wishes, she quietly yet firmly responded, "I am the Lord's servant. . . . May it be to me as you have said" (Luke 1:38).

Many of us struggle because we don't know who we are.

Teenagers especially wrestle with an identity crisis. Yet Mary knew who she was. It was already decided. She was "the Lord's servant." She had found herself by losing herself in God. She identified herself as someone who had made the Lord her master.

Mary had the heart of a servant. No wonder God was pleased!

I am also very impressed with her submissive attitude. She did not rebel against God's will, question God's plan, or try to change it. She simply said, "May it be to me as you have said."

In other words, she was saying, "What I want is God's will for my life."

She was saying, "I embrace God's will *even if . . .*"

♦ no one else will understand—and few did.
♦ Joseph leaves me—fortunately, he didn't.
♦ it is inconvenient—and what pregnancy isn't?
♦ it's not what I had planned—how could she have planned this?
♦ it will affect everything about my life for the rest of my life.
♦ it's more than I can handle—and it would be, without the Lord's help.

Wow. I am so very impressed with the level of submissiveness Mary had toward God. When confronted with God's will, she quickly, unreservedly, and totally yielded to it.

God is pleased with those who live to please Him. When we are submissive to Him, like Mary was, we are especially pleasing to God.

### TRUST IN GOD

After speaking with the angel, Mary went to share what had happened—and what was about to happen—with her elder cousin, Elizabeth. Godly Elizabeth wisely appraised Mary's situation, and was so overcome with Mary's faith that she commented: "'Blessed is she who has believed that what the Lord has said to her will be accomplished!'" (Luke 1:45).

Faith can be defined as taking God at His word. That is

exactly what Mary did. She believed that what God said to her would happen just as God said it would. If God said that Mary, a virgin, would have a baby, then Mary believed that she would have a baby. If God said that the baby would be conceived by the work of the Holy Spirit, then that's what would happen. If God said that the baby would be the Son of God, then the Son of God he would be. God said it, Mary believed it, and that settled it. Mary did not doubt it or debate it. She just believed it.

Such faith pleases God. In fact, God cannot be pleased without it (Hebrews 11:6). God's Hall of Fame is said to be in Hebrews, chapter 11. Someone observed that God's Hall of Fame could also be called God's Hall of *Faith*, because everyone mentioned in it is recognized for his or her faith.

"By faith Abel. . . . By faith Enoch. . . . By faith Noah. . . . By faith Abraham. . . . By faith Isaac. . . . By faith Jacob. . . . By faith Joseph. . . . By faith Moses' parents. . . . By faith Moses . . ." (Hebrews 11:4ff).

They were all ordinary people who did extraordinary things because they trusted God. And God was pleased with them, just as He was with Mary.

REJOICE IN GOD

And Mary said: "My soul praises the Lord and my spirit rejoices in God my Savior" (Luke 1:46–47 NIV).

And Mary said, "I'm bursting with God-news; I'm dancing the song of my Savior God" (Luke 1:46–47 THE MESSAGE).

When Mary thought of all that had happened and was about to happen, it absolutely overwhelmed her. Of all the women in her town, in her nation, on the earth at that time, and throughout all time, God had selected her to be the mother of His Son! She was not a princess or a queen. Her father wasn't the high priest. She was just a girl from an out-of-the-way town who was engaged to a carpenter. Amazing!

Mary's heart was full. She had a joy explosion of praise to God. She glorified God and rejoiced in Him as her Savior. He was indeed her all-satisfying treasure. I can see her dancing and laughing and crying all at the same time.

A joyful heart pleases God, and a heart greatly joyful in God greatly pleases God. John Piper calls it Christian hedonism, stating, "The chief end of man is to glorify God *by* enjoying Him forever."[1] He says that the bottom line in life is simply that God is most glorified in us when we are most satisfied in Him.

I have heard my wife say it many times when speaking of our children, "I just want them to be happy." All normal parents have a deep, natural yearning for the welfare and happiness of their children.

Why is God pleased when we are joyful? Why did He frequently command us to rejoice? The answer is, primarily, because God is a joyful being. Let me repeat that. God is a *joyful being.*

So often we have a misconception of God as sad, sour, and solemn. Well, certainly He is holy. And definitely, when Jesus went to the cross He was a man of sorrows. But God's dominant attitude is joy. In Hebrews 12:2 it says that it was for the *joy* that was set before Him that Jesus endured the cross. And what makes it so wonderful is that the source of His joy is . . . His children.

> The LORD your God is with you, he is mighty to save. He will take great delight in you, he will quiet you with his love, he will rejoice over you with singing" (Zephaniah 3:17).

Commenting on this verse, John MacArthur writes, "As a bridegroom rejoices over his bride the Lord will exalt over His people with gladness and song, resting in quiet ecstasy over His people in whom is all His delight."[2]

I can understand the joy of a bridegroom over his bride. I was definitely ecstatic on my wedding day. Nothing can replace the delight I felt seeing Cathy coming down the aisle, smiling at me on that happy day.

I can also understand the joy of a father over his children. If I, being an imperfect father, can so deeply delight in my three children, how much more must God, the perfect Father, delight in His! Zephaniah reminds us that when God thinks of us, all the positive emotions of a father enjoying His children are unleashed.

Zephaniah saw the Lord *in the midst of* His people. His joy-filled presence invaded their lives. When I read Zephaniah 3:17, I picture myself lying on the family room playfully wrestling *in the midst of* my three little boys when they were ages two, four, and six. I was with them, and we delighted in each other, loudly. The walls would rattle with happy squeals, laughing, hugging, tickling, and giggling. It was flat-out fun. We would make up silly songs and bellow them out at the top of our lungs. Cathy would sit on the couch and laugh along with us. We thoroughly delighted in our children. It was a joy to be so close.

God is joyful in His children too. He is pleased with us when we find our rest and joy in Him, like Mary did.

## THANK GOD

And Mary said: "My soul praises the Lord and my spirit rejoices in God my Savior, for he has been mindful of the humble state of his servant. From now on all generations will call me blessed, for the Mighty One has done great things for me—holy is his name" (Luke 1:46–49).

"God took one good look at me, and look what happened—I'm the most fortunate woman on earth! What God has done for me will never be forgotten" (Luke 1:48 THE MESSAGE).

When Mary considered the miracle of the angel appearing to her and the glorious nature of his message, her heart erupted with more than joy. It also exploded with gratitude.

◆ Mary was grateful that God noticed her.
◆ She appreciated the fact that He had chosen to bless her so extraordinarily.
◆ She was honored to think that she had been plucked from total obscurity to be remembered by all generations throughout eternity.

- ◆ She was thankful for the great miracle she was experiencing.
- ◆ She did not have a sense of entitlement that sucked all of the gratitude out of her heart.

I find that being thankful is more than a habit—it's a lifestyle. I think this psalm of glorious gratitude gushed from Mary's lips because she cultivated it in her heart. Mary lived with an all-the-time attitude of humble gratitude.

We must remember that not only is our God a joyful God but He is also a very generous God. He is a giver. Givers only want one thing from their receivers. Not guilt. Not an attempt to repay. What they want is simply a word of thanks. When we say thanks, givers receive all that they really want for their efforts. So when we are grateful for what He has done, God is pleased.

Several years ago I woke up with a flu that refused to go away. I lost 15 percent of my weight in three weeks. My joints and muscles were in incredible pain. I was completely exhausted, no matter how much I slept. Some days the best I could do was crawl down the hall to use the rest room. My throat hurt at sundown every night. Eating anything with processed sugar in it caused me to keel over. Suddenly I was allergic to a multitude of things I had never been allergic to before. When the barometer would change, I would get a migraine. I was miserable. And I did not get any better for a long, long time.

Weeks turned into months, and months turned into years. Finally I was diagnosed with Chronic Fatigue Immune Deficiency Syndrome and a severe case of metal poisoning. I ran the gauntlet of doctors' treatments and faith healers.

Eventually my illness ate away at my attitude, robbing me of my optimism. God felt far away to me, so I got discouraged and depressed.

One day my mom, who was a five-foot dynamo for God in her later years, sent me a note. At that time she had chronic pneumonia in her chest, tremors in her hands, and macular degeneration in her eyes. Her note was short and to the point: "*Quit being sorry for yourself. Thank God for what you have and get going again. Love, Mom.*"

My first reaction when I read the note was to get mad. Then I laughed and took her advice. I started a one-month fast from any prayers but ones of *gratitude*. Every time a negative thought appeared, I would start to list all the reasons I had to be thankful.

"*God, I thank you that I am not in hell. Thank you that I am not in the hospital. Thank you that I am not in jail. Thank you that I am not homeless. Thank you that I could get out of bed today.*"

And on I would go until the negative thought was gone. Within a few weeks, it became a habit, a very healthy habit. And a funny thing happened. When I got thankful, I started to get better. And God got closer. So never underestimate the power of thanksgiving. It pleases God.

RESPECT GOD

"His mercy flows in wave after wave on those who are in awe before him" (Luke 1:50 THE MESSAGE).

As Mary rejoiced in her good fortune and her mighty God, she realized a valuable truth. God's mercy flowed to her because she lived in holy awe of Him. She had a healthy fear, a holy reverence, and a deep respect for God that invited His presence into her life.

God is the most awesome being a mind can imagine. His holiness is so intense that He can literally consume everything in His blaze. He is a consuming fire (Hebrews 12:29). His throne is a giant shining rainbow of light, lightning, thunderclaps, and color (Revelation 4:2–5). Just saying His name can drop people in their tracks (John 18:6).

He alone is eternal, the first and the last, living in a perpetual present with no beginning or end. He is infinite, completely unlimited by time and space. There is nothing He does not know, nothing He has not seen, and nothing He does not comprehend. It takes words like *oceans, rivers, mountains,* and *skies* to begin to describe His love. He is awesome.

God is calmly in control of the universe. Between the parameters of sovereignty and free will, all things run according to His ultimate plan. Nothing surprises Him, worries Him, or threatens Him. He is the true center of the universe; all else circles in varying degrees of proximity to His throne.

Mary simply realized the truth. He is God, she was not; He is the potter, she was the clay; He is the shepherd, she was the sheep; He is the Master, she was a servant; He is central, she was peripheral; He is divine, she was human. As she acknowledged these facts, His presence flowed to her freely.

The bigger our view of God, the bigger God can be in our lives. The more central God is in our lives, the more His presence is manifest in our lives.

The bottom line: Mary was a God pleaser because Mary had an awesome understanding of Him. And her relationship with God and her response to Him reflected her profound gratitude for everything He had done.

Since high school I have been a God seeker. I have been blessed with a thirst for God that has never been satisfied. I have found God in some wonderful moments that I cherish as the highlights of my life. There are times I wander some, but my hunger for God always draws me back.

For me, a step of maturity has been going from living to experience God to learning to *please Him*. Mary, while still in her teens, was already a God pleaser. And because of that she got to experience Jesus like no one else in history ever did.

Let me encourage you. Be a God seeker *and* a God pleaser. Go after God with all you've got, and go for God with all you've got. It will be worth it.

### CHAPTER FIFTEEN:

# Go and Tell
## Spirit-Filled Evangelism

RECLINING AROUND THE TABLE in an upper room, Jesus shared a special meal with His twelve men. The Passover dinner was always significant, a time to remember how God had miraculously delivered His people from Egypt and how the death angel had passed over all the houses where the blood of a lamb was sprinkled on the doorframe. But tonight there was definitely something more than that to consider.

Throughout the meal Jesus was giving them solemn and significant instructions. He washed their feet and spoke of a deeper level of cleansing. Jesus discussed being betrayed. He gave them the command to love one another and said it was to be the mark of their discipleship.

Then it happened. Jesus dropped the bomb.

"My children, I will be with you only a little longer. You will look for me, and just as I told the Jews, so I tell you now: Where I am going, you cannot come" (John 13:33).

Sure, He had been alluding to it for some time. But the disciples hadn't been sure what He meant. It had seemed a long way in the future. But now the white elephant in the living room was uncovered and being discussed openly. Jesus was leaving.

The last chapter in the Jesus drama was beginning. In a few hours He would be arrested, tried, beaten, condemned, and crucified. He would resurrect from the grave and walk the earth for forty days. Then He would leave His disciples and ascend into heaven.

In His final remarks before going to the cross, Jesus shared with His disciples that even though He was departing, He would not be leaving them alone. Oh no. He would actually be leaving them *better off* than if He stayed, because He was leaving them with the expectation of a wonderful Person to come.

> "And I will ask the Father, and he will give you another Counselor to be with you forever—the Spirit of truth. The world cannot accept him, because it neither sees him nor knows him. But you know him, for he lives with you and will be in you" (John 14:16–17).

## PRINCIPLES OF THE IMMANUEL FACTOR

### 1. God's presence today is manifested in us through the Holy Spirit.

His words must have been very hard for them to comprehend: "Another Counselor"? "Be with [us] forever"? "The Spirit of truth"? "The world . . . neither sees him nor knows him"? "He lives with [us] and will be in [us]"? What on earth was Jesus talking about?

#### "ANOTHER COUNSELOR"

Jesus was telling them that the One who would replace Him in their lives would be *just like Him*. He would be *another* counselor, not a *different* counselor. The word used in the original language for *another* means "one of the same substance, the same kind."

Jesus was Immanuel, God with them. The One coming would be just like Him—that is, God with them. The Holy Spirit is part of the Trinity. He is just as much God as Jesus is God. He's as much a person as Jesus is a person. After Jesus ascended to heaven, the Holy Spirit would descend to earth to take Jesus' place as *God with us*.

### "Be With You Forever"

Jesus had walked on the earth for thirty-three and a half years. He had been with the disciples for long stretches of time as they traveled and ministered together. But all that was coming to an end. Deity incarnate in humanity had come to die for mankind's sin. He would soon ascend into heaven. He would be gone. But the coming One, who would take His place, would never need to leave. He would be with them forever.

Being a Spirit, the Holy Spirit is not limited by a human body. As God, He lives forever in a never-aging state of perfection. The disciples would never have to worry about His dying as Jesus did. And being omnipresent, they needn't worry that He would be called away on pressing business. Jesus' promise was clear: He would not leave, as Jesus was compelled to do. The Holy Spirit would remain with them *forever*.

### "The Spirit of Truth"

The age of the Spirit was dawning. God's Spirit, the Holy Spirit, was about to be given to the church. There are many names and titles given in the Bible for the Holy Spirit. They include the Spirit of Jesus Christ, Glory, Grace, and Counselor. He is called the Eternal Spirit, God, Helper, Comforter, and the third person of the Trinity. The reason He has so many titles is because He is capable of fulfilling so many roles in our lives.

But here in John 14, Jesus referred to Him as the Spirit of truth. This would be essential to the disciples because He would be the key component in helping other people understand that Jesus is the way, the truth, and the life.

### "The World Neither Sees Him nor Knows Him"

God is a spirit. He is invisible to the human eye unless He decides otherwise. Jesus is God, who became flesh and dwelt among us. But the coming One, the Spirit of truth, would not need to take on the limitations of human flesh. As a spirit, He would not be visible to the unbelieving world. But as God's Spirit, His deeds would be very evident to His children.

"HE LIVES WITH YOU AND WILL BE IN YOU"

Jesus was encouraging His protégés with the promise that when He left, the Holy Spirit would take His place. He had been God with them. Soon the Holy Spirit would be God with them. But even better than that, the Holy Spirit would be God *in* *them*, just as He is for us, with us, and in us.

As the Holy Spirit within us, He isn't bound by human limitations. He never gets hungry or thirsty. He doesn't need to go away to rest or pray. He can be with us and in us every moment for all time. Also, He is not limited to one location, as Jesus was. He can be in all of God's children, all over the planet, simultaneously.

We know that forty days after His resurrection Jesus ascended into heaven (Acts 1:10–11). A week later the Holy Spirit was given to the church. When Jesus went up, the Holy Spirit came down—and fulfilled all that Jesus promised to His first disciples.

2. **God's powerful presence is poured out on us as we step out and share the gospel.**

In both the Upper Room and the Garden of Gethsemane, Jesus gave many final instructions to His disciples. When He walked the earth for the forty days after His resurrection, Jesus shared many other lessons with His followers. But the *final* *words* He said on earth to them, and to us, are these:

"You will receive power when the Holy Spirit comes on you; and you will be my witnesses in Jerusalem, and in all Judea and Samaria, and to the ends of the earth" (Acts 1:8).

I think that in the joy of discovering the presence of God the Holy Spirit in our lives, we sometimes miss the *significance* of this event. Yes, the Holy Spirit gifts us. Yes, He teaches us, transforms us, and liberates us, but all these acts are done with one ultimate objective. God gives us the power of His presence in the person of the Holy Spirit so that we will be enabled to be *His witnesses to the world.*

## Where the Action Is

We love the comfort zone. We are enamored with convenience. We are seduced by ease. If we have to move, we love to take the route of least resistance. We are naturally passive, not active; most often we are digressing, not progressing. We tend to spiritual lethargy and laxness. And all these tendencies cause us to miss out on God.

God is not inspired to manifest His presence in our lives as we sit on the couch, remote in hand, channel surfing. He is not found as we sit and idly surf the Web. He's probably not interested when we hit the snooze button on our alarm and roll over.

God is with us when we join Him in what He is doing. And what God is doing is *actively reconciling a wicked world to himself.*

This key is seen after His resurrection, when Jesus commanded His followers to leave the sidelines and go make disciples. He promised His presence to those who obey this command.

> "Therefore go and make disciples of all nations, baptizing them in the name of the Father and of the Son and of the Holy Spirit, and teaching them to obey everything I have commanded you. And surely *I will be with you* always, to the very end of the age" (Matthew 28:19–20, emphasis added).

We all like the end of that verse, where Jesus promises to be with us till the end of the age. But too often we avoid the first part, the command to go and make disciples. Jesus did not promise one without the other. He did not pledge His presence (through the Holy Spirit) unless we are proclaiming His Word and raising up disciples. He promised to go with us as we go for Him.

## God Went With Them

Jesus' command to go and make disciples was given several times before He ascended (see John 20:21; Luke 24:47–49; Acts 1:8). "He said to them, 'Go into all the world and preach the good news to all creation'" (Mark 16:15).

And the disciples did!

Then the disciples went out and preached everywhere,
and the Lord worked with them and confirmed his word by
the signs that accompanied it. (Mark 16:20)

There is some debate over whether or not this final part of
the gospel of Mark was actually written by Mark. No matter
who penned the words, Mark or someone else, they are true.
Jesus did command His disciples to go out and proclaim the gospel, and they did. And when they did, the Lord went with them
and worked with them. That's what the book of Acts is all
about.

Peter was the first and most visible of Jesus' followers to go
boldly public with the gospel. Fifty days after Jesus was crucified, Peter stood in the courts of the temple and fearlessly pro-
claimed that Jesus had risen from the dead. God's manifest presence was so powerful that three thousand people responded to
the opportunity to repent and be baptized (Acts 2:38–41). Peter
and the other disciples continued to share the message daily, and
people continued to respond (Acts 2:47).

Later, Peter and John preached again at the temple. God
worked with them, and the total number of men who were
saved (not counting women and children) grew to five thousand
(Acts 3:11–4:4). This time their preaching led to their arrest. Yet
the presence of Jesus had transformed them and was evident in
their lives in an astonishingly real way.

When they saw the courage of Peter and John and realized that they were unschooled, ordinary men, they were
astonished and they took note that these men had been with
Jesus. (Acts 4:13)

Where did the apostles get such boldness and bravery to
preach Jesus in the same city that had crucified Him a few
months earlier? It came from being *with Jesus*.

Remarkably, this brush with persecution did not diminish
their zeal. In fact, it galvanized them. So the first thing they did
when they were released was to pray for *more boldness* to share
the word more effectively. This served to release even more of

the power of God's presence (Acts 4:23–31).

God answered their prayers, and they continued to go and tell people about Jesus with increased boldness and power. This brought additional opposition.

Then the high priest and all his associates, who were members of the party of the Sadducees, were filled with jealousy. They arrested the apostles and put them in the public jail. (Acts 5:17–18)

But God's presence attends those who are committed to sharing the Good News. In this case, He manifested His presence with the appearance of an angel.

But during the night an angel of the Lord opened the doors of the jail and brought them out. "Go, stand in the temple courts," he said, "and tell the people the full message of this new life" (Acts 5:19–20).

This miracle is mentioned in such a matter of fact manner that it's easy to overlook. Don't. Notice how God not only blessed them with deliverance but also challenged them to *keep on evangelizing*. And they were obedient.

At daybreak they entered the temple courts, as they had been told, and began to teach the people. (Acts 5:21)

While the newly released apostles were in the temple telling people about Jesus, the unsuspecting authorities gathered for their morning session. They were in for a surprise.

When the high priest and his associates arrived, they called together the Sanhedrin—the full assembly of the elders of Israel—and sent to the jail for the apostles. But on arriving at the jail, the officers did not find them there. So they went back and reported, "We found the jail securely locked, with the guards standing at the doors; but when we opened them, we found no one inside." On hearing this report, the captain of the temple guard and the chief priests were puzzled, wondering what would come of this. Then someone came and said, "Look! The men you put in jail are standing in the temple courts teaching the people" (Acts 5:21–25).

God has a great sense of humor. At the very moment the apostles were to be tried for preaching Jesus, they couldn't be found, because God helped them escape from prison and sent them to preach Jesus some more! The authorities hauled them back in. But Peter and the others were absolutely fearless as they stood before them.

> "We gave you strict orders not to teach in this name," he [the high priest] said. "Yet you have filled Jerusalem with your teaching and are determined to make us guilty of this man's blood." Peter and the other apostles replied: "We must obey God rather than men! The God of our fathers raised Jesus from the dead—whom you had killed by hanging him on a tree. God exalted him to his own right hand as Prince and Savior that he might give repentance and forgiveness of sins to Israel. We are witnesses of these things, and so is the Holy Spirit, whom God has given to those who obey him" (Acts 5:28–32).

At this, many of the authorities wanted to execute the apostles, but one wise head prevailed. Gamaliel, a Pharisee, gave this counsel:

> "I advise you: Leave these men alone! Let them go! For if their purpose or activity is of human origin, it will fail. But if it is from God, you will not be able to stop these men; you will only find yourselves fighting against God" (Acts 5:38–39).

Out of the mouths of babes and Pharisees . . . God's presence was with them, in the person of the Holy Spirit, in such a big way that to fight against them was to fight against God! Gamaliel unknowingly prophesied about their future impact. Their mission did not fail. In fact, it shook the world.

### THE SECRET OF BILLY GRAHAM'S POWER

Billy Graham is considered to be the outstanding evangelist of the twentieth century. He has preached the simple gospel of

Jesus Christ to more people in live audiences than anyone else in history—over two hundred and ten million people in more than one hundred eighty-five countries and territories, through various meetings and crusades. Hundreds of millions more have been reached through television, video, film, and Web-casts. Anyone who has heard him is captivated by the unusual power of God's manifest presence that attends his preaching. A few years ago, Billy Graham shared the secret of his amazing spiritual influence:

> In my own life there have been times when I have also had the sense of being filled with the Spirit, knowing that some special strength was added for some task I was being called upon to perform.
>
> We sailed for England in 1954 for a crusade that was to last for three months. While on the ship I experienced a definite sense of oppression. Satan seemed to have assembled a formidable array of his artillery against me. Not only was I oppressed, I was overtaken by a sense of depression, accompanied by a frightening feeling of inadequacy for the task that lay ahead. Almost night and day I prayed. I knew in a new way what Paul was telling us when he spoke about "praying without ceasing."
>
> Then one day in a prayer meeting with my wife and colleagues, a break came. As I wept before the Lord I was filled with deep assurance that power belonged to God and He was faithful. I had been baptized by the Spirit into the body of Christ when I was saved, but I believe God gave me a special anointing on the way to England. From that moment on I was confident that God the Holy Spirit was in control for the task that lay ahead. Experiences of this kind had happened to me before, and they have happened to me many times since. Sometimes no tears are shed. Sometimes as I have lain awake at night the quiet assurance has come that I was being filled with the Spirit for the task that lay ahead.[1]

God's powerful presence was poured out on Billy Graham because he accepted the challenge of sharing the gospel with the world. God's powerful presence is poured on us too when we step out and share the Good News.

### 3. God's presence is manifest mightily when we share the gospel willingly.

Powerful manifestations of the presence of God do not end with the book of Acts. In the 1800s, there was a man named Charles Finney who lived the Immanuel Factor at a level of extreme intensity. Finney was a lawyer who was dramatically converted to Christianity and immediately began to preach in small towns in upper New York State. During his God-soaked ministry over a half million souls gave themselves to Christ.

On one occasion, he had been holding a revival at New York Mills, New York, and he was asked one morning to tour the large cotton mill in town. As he walked into the mill God's manifest presence began to convict the people immediately, without Finney having to say a word. He entered a large room where the young ladies working at the looms were laughing and joking, and within minutes the room grew still. One of the girls looked into his eyes and started to tremble. Her finger began to shake and she broke her thread. Speaking of the event, Finney himself wrote,

> "She was quite overcome, and sank down, and burst into tears. The impression caught like powder and in a few moments all of the room was in tears. The feeling spread through the factory."[2]

One historian described the events with these words:

> The owner heard the equipment stopping, and came in to see what was going on. When he saw that the whole room was in tears he told the superintendent to stop the mill, for it was more important for souls to be saved than for the mill to run. Up to that point Finney had not said a word.[3]

Can you imagine? God's presence was so powerful on Finney's life that mill workers repented without his even saying a word to them. Within a few days almost all of the employees of the mill were saved.

This unusual display of the power of God was surprisingly

common in Finney's life. He lived in utter dependence on the power of God. It was not uncommon for him to spend four hours at a time seeking God in straightforward prayer. Other people were also instrumental in saturating his ministry through prayer.

In speaking of the mystery of the phenomenal power of God on Finney's life, a friend said, "It seemed to me to be always gushing up, always full. The mystery was solved when I read his memoirs. It was God in him that made him so great a blessing."[4]

### Releasing God's Presence Through Spirit-Filled Evangelism

◆ *Do ministry, don't designate ministry.*

When some people read the commands of Scripture to go and tell others about Jesus or read the exciting accounts of the apostles in the early chapters of Acts, they think that it does not apply to them. They rationalize that sharing the gospel is the job of the apostles—or in our day, the paid professionals—and has no bearing on their lives. They could not be more wrong! And they miss out on experiencing levels of the presence of God that are only realized when we share Jesus with the lost.

In the early church it would seem like the apostles did all the preaching about Jesus, but that was not so. In fact, God allowed persecution to arise to keep that from happening.

> On that day a great persecution broke out against the church at Jerusalem, and *all except the apostles* were scattered throughout Judea and Samaria. Those who had been scattered preached the word wherever they went. (Acts 8:1, 4, emphasis added)

*All except the apostles* were scattered by persecution. And all who were scattered preached the Word. This became a pivotal point in history, when the church broke out of the unfriendly confines of Jerusalem, and the ordinary believers (non-apostles) took the message of Jesus with them as they fled. At that point the church began to change from being a local entity to becoming a global reality. The only way for this to happen was for everyone to become a preacher.

Evangelistic ministry is not the exclusive domain of paid professionals. It is to be the lifestyle of all who follow Jesus and long to experience more of His presence.

Ask committed Christians when they have felt closest to God, and they will invariably say things like: through times of trial, moments in prayer, experiences in worship, and especially when they have ministered the message of Jesus to someone else.

◆ *When God says, "Go," take Him seriously.*

A few years ago Sonja was content doing the behind-the-scenes church work of a deacon's wife. But God began to take her out of her comfort zone. In fact, He took her way out of her comfort zone. The opportunity came to spend a weekend sharing Jesus at a woman's prison. Since her husband is a police officer, Sonja had a good idea about the atmosphere in most prisons, and she was understandably hesitant to even consider doing it. But God distinctly said, "Go," so she went. Later she said,

> I thought, okay, I'll go just once. Then I can say I tried and it wasn't for me. As the weekend approached the pounding in my chest increased, as did the nausea. It wasn't even thoughts of prisoners, bars, and fences; it was doubts of sharing my faith without sounding like an idiot!
>
> I went into prison that weekend, and have now gone fifteen times since. What I learned is, when God says, "Go," and we take that first step of obedience, God goes with us.

Today Sonja heads up the prison ministry in our church. Last year she even helped host a Bill Glass prison weekend in which hundreds of people went into Central Ohio prisons and shared the gospel. Dozens of inmates came to Christ each day. She loves getting others involved so they too can learn that Jesus goes to prison with us when we go to prison for Him.

◆ *Expect the Holy Spirit to be present when you talk about Jesus.*

As I have said, our family hosts a home Bible study for high school students every Wednesday night. This winter we are averaging about sixty kids each week. Believe me, our living room overflows with high school kids.

Many unchurched students have come to Christ as a result of this outreach and are now an active part of our church. We intentionally share the gospel every four or five weeks, and some kids always respond to the opportunity to be saved. Also, student leaders share the gospel with their friends as their smaller groups spread throughout the house.

A few times a year we host "Sinner Dinners" (we don't call them that publicly), where kids invite their friends. We have a ton of fun; then a few kids give their testimony, and I give an invitation. Some people always get saved as a result.

What is interesting is that the weeks we are going to present the gospel is when it is always extra crazy at my house right before the group gathers. Everyone is testy and no one seems to be able to find the things they need for the night. Usually before we are ready the kids start pouring in with their friends. It is all a little rowdy until we have some worship and corporate prayer. Then God begins to draw near. As testimonies are shared He gets closer. And when the opportunity to trust Christ is given, the room is thick with the presence of God.

Students tell me they feel closest to God when they are sharing their testimony with the larger group, or when they have brought an unsaved friend and they get to share Jesus with their friend one-on-one. You will too. God is waiting to work in and through you as you "go and tell" others about Him.

# EPILOGUE

I HOPE YOU HAVE ENJOYED the journey as we have traveled through the Bible on a quest to understand and apply the Immanuel Factor. I have to admit that I am still not where I want to be, but I am encouraged by my progress. Even more important, I am excited about my deepening relationship with Immanuel himself.

As we end this part of the trip I want to encourage you to increasingly live life in the ready awareness of the tangible presence of God. See God as *truly with you* through every moment of your day. Whether you are chasing toddlers, answering phones, doing laundry, driving a truck, running a meeting of sales reps, typing an email, teaching third graders, eating lunch with a friend, or sitting at a traffic light, see God through the eyes of faith as *actually there*—beside you, in you, and flowing through you to reach out to others.

God is looking at your heart right now and offering you an awesome opportunity. Once you decide to go through the rest of your life with Him—*really* with Him—He promises to go with you as Immanuel. His presence will only intensify as you make up your mind to stick with Him no matter what, in times of adversity and in seasons of prosperity. Determine never to leave home without Him. Make Him your magnificent obsession. Get close enough to the flame of His person that the afterglow of His glory shines all over your face.

Don't be afraid of *anything* He puts before you. He'll be there with you every step of the way. Refuse to take the credit or ever think that you can succeed on this playing field without Him. Realize that He has chosen you because you have a heart to humbly serve Him. Such service may lead into battle or through the fire, but He will go with you.

Learn to set aside serious times to invest in this, your most important relationship. Teach yourself to consciously take your quiet times with God into the noisy arena of your daily life.

When you worship, make God the focus. Don't think about what other people think. Get lost in God. Give Him the best you have. Hold nothing back. Give Him all of you—each area and every detail of your life.

Face your toughest foes and most desperate times with out-pourings of praise and gratitude. Learn to live a life of prayer. Connect with God in the morning and keep the connection open all day long.

Choose to be not only a God seeker but also a God pleaser. Make Him your greatest delight. Delight Him with your life of purity and your heart of submission. Trust Him, rejoice in Him, thank Him, and always, always give Him the utmost respect.

And don't forget to tell others about Him. This treasure of His presence must not be hoarded or it will subside. Share your treasure and you'll see it increase all the more.

The offer is made. The choice is given.

You can do it.

And you will *love it*, or my name isn't Ohio Earley.

## Endnotes

### Chapter One

1. George Barna, "Worship," *The Barna Group*, 1997, *www.barna.org/FlexPage.aspx?Page=Topic&TopicID=40* (June 13, 2005).

### Chapter Two

1. R. A. Torrey, *Why God Used D. L. Moody* (Murfreesboro, Tenn.: Sword of the Lord, 2000), 29.
2. William R. Moody, *The Life of D. L. Moody by His Son* (Murpheesboro, Tenn.: Sword of the Lord, 1900), 147.
3. Torrey, 30.

### Chapter Three

1. James Montgomery Boice, *Genesis: An Expositional Commentary*, Volume III, (Grand Rapids: Baker Books, 1987), 908–09.
2. Ibid.
3. Bruce Larson, *The Presence*, (San Francisco: Harper & Row, 1988), 75.
4. "Corrie ten Boom: The Joy-Filled Life," *Spiritual Journeys of Great Christians, In Touch Ministries*, 2005, *www.intouch.org/myintouch/mighty/ portraits/corrie_ten_boom_159770.html* (February 3, 2005).
5. From the title of the book by Eugene Peterson, *A Long Obedience in the Same Direction* (Downers Grove, Ill.: InterVarsity Press, 1980).
6. Sam Wellman, *Corrie ten Boom* (Uhrichville, Ohio: Barbour Publishing, 1995), 84.

### Chapter Four

1. Basil Miller, *John Wesley* (Minneapolis: Bethany House Publishers, 1969), 131.
2. W. Y. Fullerton, *Charles H. Spurgeon: London's Most Popular Preacher* (Chicago: Moody Press, 1966), 134.

3. Henri Nouwen as quoted by Richard Foster and James Bryan Smith in *Devotional Classics* (San Francisco: Harper Collins Publishers, 1990), 95.
4. For more on fasting, see Dave Earley, *Prayer Odyssey* (Shippensburg, Pa.: 2003), 157–62.

Chapter Five

1. "I Felt Really, Really Scared," *CNN*, Tuesday, March 15, 2005, *www. cnn.com/2005/LAW/03/14/atlanta.hostage* (March 28, 2005).
2. Arthur Lewis, *Judges and Ruth* (Chicago, Ill.: Moody Press, 1979), 45.
3. J. Vernon McGee, *Joshua and Judges* (Nashville: Thomas Nelson Publishers, 1991), 151.

Chapter Six

1. "The Re-education of Jim Bakker," *Christianity Today Library, christianitytoday.com/ct/8te/8te062.html* (November 30, 2004).
2. Ibid.
3. Clarence Edward Macartney, *Sermons on Old Testament Heroes* (Grand Rapids, Mich.: Baker Book House, 1935), 115.

Chapter Seven

1. Robert B. Munger, *My Heart, Christ's Home* (Carol Stream, Ill.: InterVarsity Press, 1954).
2. Os Hillman, "Called to Impact the Culture" from *Faith and Works: Do They Mix? Christianity 9 to 5*, 2003. *www.christianity9to5.org/articles2.cfm?article_id=53* (January 10, 2005).
3. Tim Montgomerie, "William Wilberforce: Christ in His Heart and Politics in His Blood," *Conservative Christian Fellowship, Our Worldview: Archive and Briefing, ccfwebsite.com/world_page.php?ID=22* (January 10, 2005).
4. Ibid.
5. Ibid.

Chapter Eight

1. Mother Teresa, "In Her Own Words," *Mother Teresa*, 1997. *www.drini.com/motherteresa/own_words* (October 17, 2004).
2. Mother Teresa, "In Her Own Words" *www.cnn.com/WORLD/9709/mother.teresa/quotes/index.html* (March 15, 2004).
3. Erwin Raphael McManus, *Seizing Your Divine Moment* (Nashville: Thomas Nelson, 2002), 34–35.
4. Henry Blackaby and Claude King, *Experiencing God* (Nashville: Broadman and Holman, 1998), 147–48.
5. Roland Bainton, *Here I Stand: A Life of Martin Luther* (Nashville: Abingdon Press, 1950), 144.

Chapter Nine

1. Brother Lawrence, as quoted by Harold Wiley Freer, *God Meets Us Where We Are* (Nashville: Abingdon Press, 1967), 198.
2. Brother Lawrence, *The Practice of the Presence of God* (Grand Rapids: Baker Book House, 1975), 11–24.
3. Ibid., 50.
4. Max Lucado, *Next Door Savior* (Nashville: Word Publishing Group, 2003), 128.
5. Buddy Owens, *The Way of the Worshiper* (San Clemente, Calif.: Maranatha! Publishing, 2002), 8–9.

Chapter Ten

1. Jack Taylor, *The Hallelujah Factor* (Nashville: Broadman Press, 1972), 29.
2. Philip Yancey and Tim Stafford, "Introduction to the Book of Leviticus" in *The Student Bible* (Grand Rapids: Zondervan Publishing, 1986), 127.

Chapter Eleven

1. William R. Moody, *The Life of D. L. Moody* (Murfreesboro, Tenn.: Sword of the Lord Publishers, n.d.), 134.
2. Lisa Barry, "Gladys Aylward," *Gateway to Joy, Back to the*

*Bible* (October 10, 2000): *www.backtothebible.org/gateway/ today/19328* (November 10, 2004).

Chapter Twelve

1. Greg Asimakoupoulos, "Going the Distance," pastor-port.com/msermons.asp?id=36 (July, 2004).
2. Thomas R. Kelly, *A Testament of Devotion* (San Francisco: Harper & Row, 1941), 5.
3. Ibid., 7.
4. Ibid., 16.
5. Paula Rinehart, "Effective Devotional Life" in *Discipleship Journal*, issue 24 (November 1984) at: *www.navpress.com/ Magazines/DJ/ArticleDisplay.asp?ID=eq024.1* (November 17, 2004).

Chapter Thirteen

1. Don McMinn, *Entering His Presence* (South Plainfield, N.J.: Bridge Publishing, 1986), 134.
2. Wesley Duewel, *Mighty Prevailing Prayer* (Grand Rapids: Zondervan Publishing House, 1990), 169–70.
3. Watchman Nee, *Assembling Together* (New York: Christian Fellowship Publishers, 1973), 116.
4. Ibid.
5. Story adapted from Olive Fleming Liefeld, *Unfolding Destinies* (Grand Rapids: Zondervan, 1990).

Chapter Fourteen

1. John Piper, *Desiring God* (Portland, Ore.: Multnomah, 1986), 14.
2. John MacArthur, *John MacArthur Study Bible* (Nashville: Word Bibles, 1997), 1330.

Chapter Fifteen

1. Billy Graham as quoted by Elmer Towns, *Understanding the Deeper Life* (Old Tappan, N.J.: Revell, 1988), 214–15.

2. Basil Miller, *Charles Finney* (Minneapolis: Bethany House Publishers, 1969), 55.
3. Wesley Duewel, *Revival Fires* (Grand Rapids: Zondervan, 1995), 103.
4. Miller, 131.